Executives in Crisis

Jeffrey Lynn Speller

Executives in Crisis

Recognizing and Managing the Alcoholic, Drug-Addicted, or Mentally Ill Executive

Jossey-Bass Publishers

San Francisco • London • 1989

EXECUTIVES IN CRISIS
Recognizing and Managing the Alcoholic, Drug-Addicted, or Mentally Ill Executive
by Jeffrey Lynn Speller

Copyright © 1989 by: Jossey-Bass Inc., Publishers
350 Sansome Street
San Francisco, California 94104
&
Jossey-Bass Limited
28 Banner Street
London EC1Y 8QE

Library of Congress Cataloging-in-Publication Data

Speller, Jeffrey Lynn, date.
    Executives in crisis : recognizing and managing the alcoholic,
drug-addicted, or mentally ill executive / Jeffrey Lynn Speller.
        p.   cm. — (Jossey-Bass management series) (Jossey-Bass
social and behavioral science series)
    Bibliography: p.
    Includes index.
    ISBN 1-55542-175-X
    1. Problem employees. 2. Employee assistance programs.
3. Executives—Drug use. 4. Executives—Alcohol use.
5. Executives—Mental health. I. Title. II. Series. III. Series:
Jossey-Bass social and behavioral science series.
HF5549.5.E42S63   1989
658.3′045-dc20   89-45571
                                                           CIP

Manufactured in the United States of America

The paper in this book meets the guidelines for
permanence and durability of the Committee on
Production Guidelines for Book Longevity of the
Council on Library Resources.

JACKET DESIGN BY WILLI BAUM

FIRST EDITION

Code 8949

A joint publication in
The Jossey-Bass Management Series
and
The Jossey-Bass Social and Behavioral Science Series

Contents

ix

Contents

Preface

Alcoholism, drug abuse, and mental illness can have a devastating impact. An article in the *New York Times* business section began this way:

> At 33, Bill O'Donnell Jr. had succeeded. He was vice president of Bally Manufacturing, had an annual salary of $150,000, owned two Mercedes Benz's and an expensive house in Winnetka, Illinois.
> He also cheated on his wife, missed meetings he had called and used 4 grams of cocaine a day [Goleman, 1986, p. 1F].

Although alcoholism, drug abuse, and mental illness can strike anyone, the potential effect of one or more of these conditions on an upper-level or senior executive is much greater than that on an hourly employee, supervisory manager, or middle manager. Alcoholic, drug-abusive, or mentally ill senior executives are very costly to all organizations, whether private or public, large or small. They make bad decisions, irritate and frustrate their colleagues, lose sight of priorities, miss deadlines, forget important assignments, lower morale, act impulsively, and think irrationally. Although the number of senior executives in any given firm who are troubled by addictions or mental illness may be small, even one seriously disturbed senior executive whose condition goes undetected and untreated can cost an organization hundreds of thousands of dollars in bad decisions and can adversely affect the productivity and competitiveness of the firm as a whole. In addition, the costs of recruiting, hiring, training, and developing a replacement for a highly experienced and capable senior executive—not to mention the disability retirement and continuing health care costs—can also be quite significant for the organization.

The eventual personal cost to the untreated alcoholic, drug-dependent, or mentally ill senior executive and his or her family can also be very great: the loss of a stable means of financial support, the end of a career, and the disruption of the family. But if these senior executives are identified and successfully treated early in the course of their illness, then many of them can return to productive and satisfying careers.

The challenge of detecting and managing the alcoholic, drug-dependent, or mentally ill upper-level executive is a reality for all organizations, regardless of size or type of business. No one is immune. Many corporations have already realized the importance of an aggressive approach to the problem of blue-collar and white-collar employee addictions and mental illness. During the last ten years many firms have initiated employee-assistance programs (EAPs) that have targeted these employee groups. Many firms have established and maintain in-house staffs of medical and nursing professionals and alcohol and drug-abuse counselors who assist the troubled blue-collar or white-collar employee. Many of these firms have experienced significant success in dealing with and managing alcoholic, drug-abusive, or mentally ill blue-collar workers, supervisors, and middle managers, but in many cases impaired senior executives have remained unaffected by the best efforts of these firms.

Why? The most common reasons include (1) the frequent lack of close, day-to-day supervision of senior executives by their superiors, (2) the difficulty in connecting a developing health problem with the impairment of day-to-day performance, particularly in the early phases of the illness, (3) the desire by loyal subordinates to cover up for a senior executive's impairment, and (4) the absence of senior colleagues who are aware of the impaired executive's problems and who have sufficient status, desire, and knowledge to confront and follow through with the executive.

Thus, the problem continues. Over the years I have counseled a number of executives who were in trouble in this way. Some of their comments are presented below:

> A senior vice-president of personnel, and a recovering alcoholic himself, stated, "The number of active alcoholics in the senior management ranks in this company is astounding, yet only one in ten is willing to get help."

> "When I went for treatment for my cocaine problem, my fellow coke users in the corporation thought that I was crazy to risk my career by admitting my problem." This is a senior vice-president of marketing from a mid-sized high-technology firm in California.

> A fifty-six-year-old senior executive who was a heavy drinker for more than thirty years finally realized he was in trouble. "My alcohol problem was so bad that I needed three strong drinks before work in the morning just to make it through to lunch, but no one at work suspected that I had a problem until it was nearly too late."

> From a forty-six-year-old senior executive in government who went through a painful and difficult divorce: "I knew I was developing a serious problem with depression when I started seriously thinking about jumping out of my sixth-story window, while all the time I maintained a cool and calm facade in the office—no one ever knew I was thinking about killing myself."

> "Although I'm a manic-depressive, not even my closest colleagues at work suspected that I had any problems—that is, until I stopped taking my lithium carbonate and

became psychotic," explained a forty-two-year-old hospitalized upper-level executive who was recovering from a
manic episode.

Audience

Executives in Crisis is for those executives, human resource
managers, and personnel officers who, lacking the benefit of
professional advice, well-formulated policies, and clearly established procedures, have been struggling to deal with their impaired upper-level executives on a case-by-case basis, often with
mixed results. Although the impaired senior executive may be a
rarity at many firms, all organizations, large or small, greatly depend on *all* their senior executives to guide the firm through today's turbulent marketplace. In many organizations the impairment of a crucial senior executive can literally threaten the very
existence of the business.

The purpose of this book is to help the reader recognize
the early symptoms and, thereby, effectively manage alcoholism,
drug addiction, or mental illness among senior executives. This
objective is accomplished in several ways. *Executives in Crisis*
(1) increases the reader's awareness of the problems of alcoholic,
drug-addicted, and mentally ill senior executives; (2) reviews for
the reader the basic concepts of alcoholism, drug dependency,
and mental illness and relates them to the disturbed senior executive; (3) teaches the reader how to recognize the early warning
signs of alcoholism, drug abuse, or mental illness in the impaired
senior executive; (4) instructs the reader on how to get an impaired upper-level executive into treatment and keep him or her
there; (5) helps the reader manage the treated or rehabilitated
senior executive once he or she returns to work; and (6) instructs
the reader in the development of organizational strategies that
effectively deal with the impaired senior executive. In each
chapter the basic concepts are stated clearly in nontechnical lan-
guage and brought to life through case histories and clinical
vignettes.

Although the basic concepts of the detection and treatment of alcoholism, drug abuse, and mental illness have been in

existence for some time, *Executives in Crisis* applies these concepts to senior executives in a comprehensive and systematic way, thereby broadening the base of knowledge and practice of human resources management. Alcoholism, drug abuse, and mental illness can strike anyone from the chairman of the board to the hourly employee, but the problems of detecting and treating seriously disturbed upper-level executives are different and require a different approach.

Because this book is a practical guide that gives concrete advice, it is very different from other books currently available on the topics of the psychology of the executive (Levinson, 1964, 1981; Kets de Vries and Miller, 1984; Grieff and Munter, 1980; Maccoby, 1981; Kotter, 1982; Rohrlich, 1980) and executive stress (Blotnick, 1984; Cooper and Marshall, 1977; Cooper and Payne, 1980; Levinson, 1975; McLean, 1974). Many of these works focus on the manager or executive who may be troubled by a variety of personal problems, including legal and financial difficulties, supervisor-peer-subordinate conflicts, family and marital problems, neurotic conflicts, "burnout," work overload, and stress. Although these works are important and helpful, the executive, manager, or personnel officer who is looking for an easy-to-read text that specifically addresses the problems of dealing with the addicted or mentally ill senior executive will be disappointed. *Executives in Crisis* focuses on a group of senior executives who go beyond the bounds of neurotic illness, stress reactions, or adjustment difficulties and develop serious problems with alcoholism, drug abuse, depression, mania, or psychosis, usually requiring a period of hospitalization.

The idea for this book came from my experience in consulting to private industries and government about emotionally impaired executives and employees. During the course of these consultations a number of executives, managers, and personnel officers commented that they suspected that there were more executives having difficulty with drugs, alcohol, or mental illness, particularly at the upper levels, than were currently seeking help. For some of these employers, the first indication they had that their upper-level executives might be having such a problem came when, without warning, a senior executive became acutely ill, requiring immediate hospitalization. When the treated senior executive returned to work, the employer was unsure of what to expect or how to proceed in making the reentry process as smooth as possible. In other cases, the signs that things were not going well with an upper-level executive came in the form of persistent complaints from clerical staff or other executives that this individual had been behaving inappropriately—in some cases for years—or simply not performing up to his or her potential. Many of these employers sought my advice on how and when to intervene. In the course of assisting these employers, I learned a great deal about how to detect the early warning signs and how to manage the seriously disturbed senior executive before, during, and after treatment.

In addition, I have treated on an outpatient or inpatient basis a number of alcoholic, drug-addicted, or mentally ill executives who admitted that they did not realize they were having a serious problem, particularly with drugs or alcohol, in the early stage of their illness. These senior executives were reluctant and resistant to seeking help because they were fearful, embarrassed, or simply unsure of how to seek help. In treating them, I have gained a better understanding of why it is often difficult for anyone—executive, manager, or personnel officer—to detect and assist these individuals and have developed strategies to effectively deal with the reluctant or resistant impaired senior executive.

Overview of the Contents

Executives in Crisis is divided into three sections. In Part One, Chapters One and Two describe the problem of the impaired senior executive; present a definition of an impaired senior executive; discuss the issue of the impaired woman or minority executive; define mental health and mental illness; describe the financial impact of alcoholism, drug addiction, or mental illness on the executive and the company; and discuss the causes of alcoholism, drug abuse, and mental illness.

Part Two deals with the problems of detecting the impaired senior executive by focusing on the signs and symptoms of alcoholism, drug abuse, and mental illness in the senior executive ranks. This section will be of particular interest to those readers who have only a casual knowledge or understanding of these problems. (The more sophisticated reader may want to turn directly to Part Three, which describes in detail the strategies for managing the alcoholic, drug-addicted, or mentally ill senior executive.) In Chapters Three, Four, Five, Six, and Seven, the reader is introduced to five major senior executive illnesses: alcoholism, drug abuse, depression, mania, and psychosis. The chapters contain case histories of senior executives who got into trouble with each of these conditions. Each chapter discusses the nature of one illness, briefly discusses its causes, and emphasizes its early warning signs.

Part Three describes in detail the strategies for successfully managing the alcoholic, drug-addicted, or mentally ill senior executive. Chapter Eight describes the steps to determine whether a given executive is impaired and in need of treatment, including collecting, reviewing, and evaluating data on the executive's job performance; consulting with a mental health professional about tentative conclusions; and confronting the impaired executive about his or her deteriorating job performance. In addition, the chapter describes what to do if an executive acutely decompensates and what to do to keep an impaired executive in treatment.

Chapter Nine discusses managing the rehabilitated or recovering executive once he or she returns to work. The reader is instructed in the specific steps to take to ensure a smooth and successful reintegration into the firm, including meeting with the recovering executive before discharge from the treatment facility, developing an appropriate and individualized aftercare plan, making temporary or permanent adjustments in the returning executive's job routines and responsibilities, preparing the corporate staff for the recovering executive's return to work, planning for the possibility of relapse, and scheduling regular meetings with the executive after his or her return to work. In addition, the chapter discusses specific aftercare strategies for the recovering alcoholic or drug-addicted executive. Support services for the executive's family are also described, and specific suggestions are given for how to deal with the executive who either relapses or cannot return to work. The chapter ends with a discussion of when to fire an impaired senior executive.

Chapter Ten offers a set of suggestions for developing a corporate policy and set of procedures that will ensure the early detection, treatment, and reintegration of the recovering senior executive into the firm. The focus is on the why, what, where, and for whom of corporate policy. An example of a corporate policy on the impaired senior executive is presented.

Chapter Eleven covers a variety of issues, including selecting a mental health consultant, identifying specific treatment resources in the community of the troubled executive, training executives in proper procedures in the management of the impaired executive, reviewing company policy on sick leave and adjusting company disability and group health insurance policies, and developing an evaluation procedure to monitor the success of efforts to detect and manage the troubled executive.

Chapter Twelve presents case studies from three organizations that struggled to manage the impaired senior executive. The chapter focuses on their efforts and offers suggestions for how things could have been handled differently.

Chapter Thirteen concludes the book by putting the challenge of managing the impaired senior executive in perspective. The chapter reflects on the drawbacks and limitations of the approach advocated throughout the book.

The Resource provides useful information about psychotherapy and psychiatric medication.

It is my hope that everyone concerned with helping seriously disturbed senior executives will benefit from reading this book, although it is not intended as the definitive work on the subject. It is a result of my unique clinical and consulting experiences. Although I was trained as a physician and psychiatrist, my approach is eclectic, with a perspective gained from disciplines including clinical psychiatry, psychology, social work, general management, organizational development and behavior, and human resources and personnel management. I attempt to take a balanced view by focusing on both the disturbed senior executive's behavior and his psyche, while emphasizing the importance of structures within the environment to help detect symptoms and appropriately manage these individuals before, during, and after their treatment. For example, I emphasize the importance of self-help programs, including Alcoholics Anonymous, Narcotics Anonymous, and Emotions Anonymous (AA, NA, and EA), in the early detection of senior executives who may be in the beginning stages of relapse, as an integral part of the inpatient or outpatient treatment plan, and as an effective follow-up and aftercare plan to prevent relapse.

In the book I have taken the position that alcoholism and drug addiction are diseases. In doing this, I am being consistent with the long-held policies of the American Medical Association, the American Hospital Association, and the AFL-CIO. Some readers will disagree, preferring to view alcoholism and drug abuse not as illnesses but as a result of willful misconduct, a lapse in moral judgment, or stresses within the work and home environments. Seeing these conditions as diseases does not imply that they can or should only be detected or treated by a physician. Quite the contrary—some of the best remedies for these problems are not physician oriented—for example, AA, NA, and EA; freestanding alcohol-rehabilitation centers; drug-free treatment programs; and substance-abuse halfway and quarterway houses. When I use the term *disease*, I am trying to convey the idea that alcoholism and drug addiction are serious conditions, largely out of the individual's control, that require intensive, continuous, and long-term intervention or monitoring. There are no "cured" substance abusers, only "recovering" alcoholics or drug addicts.

Because of the limitations of space I present only five executive illnesses. Although these illnesses are the ones that I have encountered most often in my consultation with executives, they are, by no means, the only illnesses that afflict senior executives. Like everyone, executives can be struck down unexpectedly by a large number of emotional, psychiatric, and physical illnesses. The framework presented in this book is not the only way to view senior executives in crisis, nor are my suggestions for managing them necessarily new or unique. There is and will always be healthy debate about the best way to understand and effectively manage the mentally ill. This framework has helped me assist troubled senior executives in a wide range of organizations, and I believe it will also help readers in their struggle with troubled senior executives.

Special Note About Case Histories and Use of Terms

I have used a number of terms throughout the text to describe the emotional turmoil of the troubled senior executive. The terms *psychiatric illness, psychiatric disorder, mental illness, emotional distress, emotional upset, psychological distress,* and *psychiatric disease* are used interchangeably and refer to any of a broad range of psychiatric disorders and disturbed states of mind as defined in *Diagnostic and Statistical Manual of Mental Disorders–III–Revised,* otherwise referred to as the DSM–III–R (American Psychiatric Association, 1987). The terms *alcoholism, alcohol abuse, alcohol addiction, drug addiction, illicit drug use, drug abuse, drug dependency, substance abuse, substance dependency, chemical abuse, chemical dependency,* and *chemical addiction* refer to a subset of psychiatric disorders referred to as *substance-use disorders* in the DSM–III–R.

All case histories and vignettes in the text are composites of clinical material collected from a wide variety of sources. Senior executives and other individuals presented in the text are fictional. Any similarity of characters presented in the text to any person living or dead is purely coincidental. This text was not intended for and should not be used by a lay person to make formal diagnoses and determine treatment. The proper use of criteria for diagnosis and treatment requires specialized clinical training that provides a body of knowledge and clinical skills. An experienced mental health professional should always be consulted when seeking a formal diagnosis and treatment recommendation.

Acknowledgments

I am intellectually and emotionally indebted to the many individuals who made this book possible. First and foremost are my patients and clients, the executives who have been afflicted with alcoholism, drug addiction, and mental illness, who must remain anonymous. To them I owe perhaps the greatest debt. They have taught me a great deal as I have attempted to help them. This book is dedicated to them. Robert Hargrove of Hargrove Associates offered invaluable advice, as did Peter Brill, Barrie Greiff, David Morrison, David Robbins, and Jay Rohrlich. I would like to express my gratitude to three of my teachers, Frances K. Millican, David Raphling, and Joseph H. Smith of the Washington Psychoanalytic Institute, for the invaluable clinical advice they have provided over the years. John S. Kafka, also of the Washington Psychoanalytic Institute, was instrumental in supporting me and giving me the courage to persevere. I am indebted to Manfred Kets de Vries, Harry Levinson, Michael Maccoby, and Abraham Zaleznik, all pioneers in the application of psychoanalysis to the study of organizations, who over the years have played important mentor roles. Finally, special thanks belong to my wife, Tanya Korkosz, whose helpful comments and overall support have made this book possible.

Cambridge, Massachusetts   Jeffrey Lynn Speller
August 1989

The Author

Jeffrey Lynn Speller is executive director of the Leadership Research Project and lecturer in the Department of Psychiatry, Cambridge Hospital, Harvard Medical School, Harvard University. The Leadership Research Project is an interdisciplinary research program dedicated to the study of leadership in business, government, labor, health care, and education. Speller received a B.A. degree (1970) in philosophy from Haverford College, an M.D. degree (1974) from the Harvard Medical School, and an M.B.A. degree (1979) from Harvard Business School. He completed his psychiatric residency (1975-1978) at McLean Hospital, Harvard Medical School. He is a former candidate for the doctorate in business administration degree (1981-1982) at the George Washington University School of Business and Public Administration. He completed his training for the certificate in psychoanalysis from the Washington Psychoanalytic Institute in 1988. He is a practicing psychiatrist and psychoanalyst.

Speller's main research interest lies in the interface between psychoanalysis, occupational and industrial psychiatry, and organizational behavior and management policy. Specific areas of interest are leadership, organizational dynamics, organizational and executive stress, and executive development. He has published several scientific papers as chapters in books and as articles in journals.

Speller is the founder of the Cambridge Institute, a management consulting firm and private psychiatric group practice specializing in problems of leadership, executive and employee performance, and human resources management. Former clients have included AT&T; IBM; Arthur Anderson; National Medical Enterprises; and the United States Departments of State, Defense, Commerce, Labor, and Health and Human Services.

Executives in Crisis

1

~~~~~~

Why Impaired Executives
Often Go
Undetected and Untreated

Now is a very difficult time to be a senior executive. The proliferation of mergers, acquisitions, divestitures, hostile takeovers, and leveraged buyouts has put tremendous pressure on executives to do a better job to remain competitive in the international economy. Cutbacks, layoffs, and consolidations in the name of "restructuring" are becoming a way of life, as executives are forced to drastically cut costs and raise quarterly earnings to boost stock prices. No longer can executives count on a comfortable and secure thirty-year career with the same firm. Challenge, change, and adaptation are the new bywords for the 1990s and beyond. In this new environment it is crucial that employers hire, retain, and develop executives who are psychologically stable, highly productive, motivated, and committed to organizational goals. An optimally functioning senior executive group is an employer's most important resource and most powerful competitive weapon. Without it, the organization is doomed to fail. But senior executives, like every other important asset, need constant attention and care. Firms no longer have the luxury of having a member of the senior management team not do his or her share. Senior executives who become alcoholic, drug abusive, or mentally ill are a threat to the productive effort of the organization as a whole. It is also no longer acceptable, useful, or wise to wait for a senior executive who is at risk for the development of psychological distress to completely "fall apart" before anyone intervenes. Without attention, executives in crisis usually get worse, not better. A proactive rather than a reactive strategy simply makes more sense.

Fortunately, the intense media coverage of the problems of alcoholism, drug abuse, and mental illness in society as a whole and in the work place in particular has helped bring these issues into the public's awareness. Articles in the popular press, television "specials" on drug abuse and addiction, and commercials by mental health facilities extolling the virtues of their alcohol- or drug-treatment program all have increased the general level of awareness of these problems. As a consequence, over the course of the last decade most employers have begun to take a more aggressive approach to the problem of blue-collar and white-collar employee drug abuse, alcoholism, and mental illness. Employers today now recognize that simply identifying and firing the "bad apples" is not the answer. Replacing a previously effective, knowledgeable, and experienced employee is expensive—costs include those for recruitment, training, and, in some cases, legal fees to defend the organization against wrongful-discharge suits. Given the increasingly competitive and demanding marketplace, employers are under greater pressure to hire and retain employees who are productive, committed to organizational objectives, and emotionally stable.

Because of this new perspective, an increasing number of professionals well versed in the concepts of alcoholism, drug abuse, and mental illness are finding employment as human resource managers, substance-abuse counselors, and employee-assistance counselors within large organizations. Employee-assistance programs (EAPs), designed to detect and deal with the impaired employee, are now a fixture in many institutions. Many firms also maintain in-house staffs of medical and nursing professionals and alcohol- and drug-abuse counselors. Because of these efforts, many firms have experienced significant success in dealing with and managing the alcoholic, drug-abusing, or mentally ill blue-collar worker, supervisor, or middle manager.

Yet, in spite of all these programs, the impaired upper-level executive continues to elude the best efforts of many firms.

Over the years an increasing number of employers have voiced to me their concern that their early warning systems for identifying impaired employees were not detecting upper-level executives impaired by alcoholism, drug abuse, or mental illness. This sentiment is also held by the academic community. Shain and Groeneveld (1980) report, "There is a substantial body of opinion which holds that EAP does not reach corporate executives or indeed a major portion of white-collar, highly skilled employees" (p. 126). A study by Trice and Beyer (1977) reported that executive and other highly skilled employees in federal installations were less frequently approached by their superiors with the aim of a referral to an EAP.

Why is this? There are a number of reasons. First, the vast majority of senior-level executives in our public and private institutions are white, married, well educated, and male—a group that traditionally becomes psychologically impaired much less often than the population as a whole. Successfully "climbing the ladder" in today's highly competitive marketplace is an enormous challenge requiring one's full emotional, intellectual, psychological, and physical energies. As one senior executive said, "The corporate suite is no place for amateurs." There is little room for or tolerance of executives who can't "cut the mustard" for whatever reason, for example, emotional impairment or, more commonly, simple managerial incompetence. Many senior managers are probably correct in their belief, stated succinctly by one senior vice-president of marketing, that "on the whole, we are probably tougher, stronger, and healthier than the average person." Many of these senior executives believe that they come from stronger, more stable backgrounds and that they have good marriages and good support systems that allow them to deal with the stresses of the corporate world. They also believe that they have been toughened by the process of the climb up the corporate ladder and have learned to deal successfully with the tensions and pressures of corporate life.

Second, many senior executives, because of the nature of their position and job responsibilities, lack close day-to-day supervision. Many senior executives exercise great latitude in their jobs. They can structure their daily activities and manage their time as they see fit. They can come and go as they wish. There is no one looking over their shoulder every moment of the day closely monitoring their behavior and performance. As a consequence, day-to-day executive accountability is difficult, if not impossible, to establish. In addition, there may be very few colleagues in the firm who have the sufficient status, supervisory authority, desire, or knowledge to confront and follow through if they suspect that a senior executive is becoming impaired.

Third, loyal subordinates, out of a misplaced desire to be helpful, may cover up for a senior executive's impairment. No one, particularly loyal subordinates, likes to admit that the "chief" is ill and in need of professional help. More commonly, subordinates will hope that their boss's current impairment is a temporary phenomenon that will go away quickly. Thus, subordinates will cover up for the chief's mistakes and inappropriate behavior to allow him time to "pull himself together." Unfortunately, in this scenario things usually go from bad to worse as the senior executive becomes increasingly impaired while being deprived of the early professional intervention that could be so helpful.

Fourth, the high compensation of senior executives may, paradoxically, contribute to their impairment. The alcoholic or drug-addicted senior executive is different from the average chemically dependent individual in that high income allows him or her to continue the habit without major financial strain, at least in the early stages of the illness. Some of these impaired executives even view their excessive alcohol consumption or drug use as an "earned right" in exchange for accepting the inherent stresses in the corporate life-style or as a reward for their years of sacrifice and hard work while climbing the corporate ladder.

Those few troubled executives who admit to their illness and seek help are able to use their considerable financial resources to purchase private professional help. All professional treatment is confidential. Troubled executives and the treating professionals are under no obligation to report the occurrence of such treatment to corporate management. A number of executives pay for their treatment completely out of pocket rather than use their company-sponsored health insurance policy because they are afraid of alerting their corporate peers to their problem. This behavior, although understandable, deprives the organization of learning about and understanding the difficulties its executives may be having, making it difficult to develop organizationwide policies and procedures that might help avoid such problems.

Fifth, many senior executives view asking for help as a sign of weakness. A number of senior executives believe that they must maintain an image of toughness in order to justify their own high status and position within the firm. Because of the societal stigma attached to alcoholism, drug abuse, and mental illness, many senior executives believe that any sign of weakness or distress would "open the door" to rivals within the firm. As one CEO put it, "The sharks are always circling. Once they smell blood, you're dead." The executive's fear of reprisals if his or her need for help became known contributes to a deepening sense of isolation and estrangement from helping professionals.

Sixth, senior executives resist using corporate-sponsored programs that traditionally have served blue-collar, supervisory management, and even middle-management employees. Many senior executives have the mistaken belief that what may be good for their subordinates may not necessarily be good for themselves. As one executive vice-president put it, "I pay those guys' salaries [referring to his firm's in-house EAP professionals]. They work for me. I will be d——ed if I'll now turn around and go down and ask them for help." Senior executives have been known to avoid their own in-house professional help because of fear of the possible breach of confidentiality or concern about "inverting" the traditional and clearly defined superior-subordinate roles in the firm.

Given the above reasons, it is clear why the impaired senior executive may elude the best efforts of the firm's early warning systems for the detection of alcoholism, drug abuse, and mental illness. Even when a boss becomes aware that an executive has a serious problem with alcohol, drugs, or mental illness, the boss may demand that the troubled executive simply "get her or his act together" but may not provide appropriate resources or support to make this possible. It then comes as no surprise when the boss, increasingly frustrated as the troubled executive fails to "shape up," fires the individual. Although there are circumstances when it becomes to important to "cut one's losses" and release an impaired senior executive (more will be said about this in a later chapter), a precipitous firing without adequate attention to the impaired executive's needs, both present and future, usually helps no one.

There are many employers who are sincerely motivated to assist their senior executives but lack knowledge of how best to handle the situation. They do not know what to do or how to do it. The uninformed but well-meaning employer who sincerely tries to help may end up making the situation worse for everyone. Common mistakes include giving the troubled executive time off from work to "relax" rather than recommending professional help, trying to assume the role of psychiatrist or counselor, and recommending a reassignment or change in responsibilities rather than professional treatment. Given the above reasons, any corporate program specifically designed to assist the impaired senior executive must take into account both the needs and concerns of the employer and the needs and resistances of the impaired senior executive.

Who Is the Troubled Executive?

Who is the troubled upper-level executive? The alcoholic, drug-abusing, or mentally ill senior executive can be anyone—from the chairman of the board to the divisional vice-president. Alcoholism, drug abuse, and mental illness do not discriminate. The high status, native intelligence, years of dealing with the day-to-day stresses of corporate life, and strong family support systems, although important, do not confer any immunity on senior executives with regard to the development of these illnesses. Hence, troubled upper-level executives come from all types of companies—large and small, public and private; from government and private industry; from manufacturing and service companies; and from high-tech firms and basic industries. Troubled senior executives come in all sizes, shapes, races, and religions and from all parts of the country. They are male or female, young or old, white or black, newly hired or old-timers, and high school graduates or holders of Ph.D. degrees. Troubled upper-level executives can be research and development directors, vice-presidents of marketing, executive vice-presidents, chief financial officers, chief executive officers, senior vice-presidents for manufacturing, small-business owners, heads of high-tech companies, managing partners of Wall Street investment banking firms, senior vice-presidents for personnel, and senior managers in government.

What does trouble look like in an upper-level executive? Much the same as it does in the blue-collar or middle-management employee. Trouble comes in all forms. Complicating the picture is the fact that many seriously impaired senior executives as well as their impaired subordinates will still have periods when their behavior and performance appear quite normal, appropriate, and acceptable. The crucial difference between the emotionally stable individual and the troubled individual, whether a blue-collar worker or a senior vice-president, is that the troubled individual stops functioning—professionally and personally. Sigmund Freud said that the mark of mental health was the ability to work and love. Troubled individuals can do neither. During periods of stress and crisis the mentally healthy individual bounces back from unexpected setbacks and masters challenge. The troubled individual does not. Instead of bouncing back, the troubled individual comes unraveled. Troubled individuals may lose touch with their surroundings. They may become unpredictable and behave strangely and inappropriately. They may become overwhelmed and unable to manage intense and painful feelings. They may become inappropriately aggressive or unexplainably withdrawn. They may forget things. They may overreact to situations. They may lose their sense of humor. They may become suspicious and distrustful. They may lose touch with reality. They may become apathetic and pessimistic. They may lose their intellectual sharpness, their political savvy, their good business sense. Their judgment may deteriorate, and they may lose their insight. They may become indecisive, and their thinking may become confused. They may lose all sense of perspective and misinterpret events in their environment. The following brief vignettes are but a few examples of senior executives who have gotten into trouble:

> Jim, a forty-two-year-old M.B.A. graduate from a prestigious business school and a Wall Street investment banking partner, became addicted to cocaine and began selling inside information to help support his habit.

> Barney, a senior vice-president of a manufacturing firm, drank nearly two fifths of hard liquor a day. Barney was caught embezzling funds from various corporate accounts.

> Fran, a very successful senior account executive for a financial services corporation, divorced her husband after sixteen years. Shortly after signing the divorce papers, she attempted suicide by overdosing on aspirin.

> Bill, a decorated Vietnam veteran and forty-four-year-old senior vice-president for marketing for a manufacturing firm, had a long history of persecutory feelings but had always refused counseling. He got into an argument with his boss one day and was fired. The next day he returned to work with three semiautomatic weapons and fatally shot his boss and six other executives before putting a gun to his own head and pulling the trigger.

> Harry, a sixty-two-year-old certified public accountant and senior executive for a family-owned firm, lost his wife to breast cancer after a long and difficult struggle. Three months after the funeral Harry began speaking rapidly, spending money freely, giving expensive presents to complete strangers, and making long-distance calls to the heads of various European countries. He was admitted to a psychiatric hospital after he punched the maitre d' at an expensive restaurant for seating him at a table with poor lighting.

> Jerry, a fifty-year-old senior vice-president of finance at a medium-sized firm, had a teenage son who committed

suicide. Several months after the funeral Jerry complained that other executives in the company were plotting to replace him, that his telephone was tapped, that members of a terrorist group were attempting to kill him, and that someone was putting powerful mind-altering drugs in his food.

Walter, the seventy-three-year-old founder and chairman of the board of a regional retailing chain, began to forget board-meeting times as well as important items on the meeting agenda. He would go over issues resolved in previous meetings and would call board members by the wrong names. He minimized his problem, refused to seek medical or psychiatric care, and refused to discuss plans for retirement.

Margaret, a fifty-three-year-old senior vice-president of personnel and the first woman in the company to attain senior executive status, began to have trouble with her new twenty-six-year-old assistant vice-president. Margaret thought that her assistant was plotting to replace her, believed that her phone was tapped, and thought that strangers on the street were talking about her behind her back.

Are Senior Women or Minority Executives at Risk?

What about the impaired senior executive who is a woman or a member of a minority group? Unfortunately, there continue to be too few of these individuals, healthy or impaired, in positions of senior responsibility and leadership in the country's public and private institutions. Their absence from the corporate suite is a tragedy in and of itself. Nevertheless, are women and minority senior executives who become impaired in any way different from their white, male counterparts? Or are women and minority senior executives more at risk or less so for the development of alcoholism, drug abuse, or mental illness? Although these are important questions, the number of women and minority senior executives is, as yet, too small to draw any conclusions.

Summary

In this section I have briefly introduced the magnitude of the problem of alcoholism, drug abuse, and mental illness in the work place and particularly within the senior executive ranks. I have made the point that although alcoholism, drug abuse, and mental illness are no different in their impact on the blue-collar worker and on the senior executive, the early warning systems of many firms are not detecting the impaired senior executive. I have delineated the reasons for this and have emphasized that any corporate program designed to detect and effectively deal with alcoholic, drug-abusive, or mentally ill senior executives must take into account the unique needs, concerns, and resistances of this group. The following chapter introduces the definition, cost, and causes of alcoholism, drug abuse, and mental illness.

2

Costs and Causes of Executive Alcoholism, Drug Abuse, and Mental Illness

What Are Mental Health and Mental Illness?

Exactly what constitutes mental health or mental illness? It is indeed a difficult question to answer. Although psychiatry is a respected subspecialty of medicine, a clear definition of mental illness remains elusive. Many psychiatric disorders overlap (American Psychiatric Association, 1987) and the reasons for their onset are still obscure. The cures are even more uncertain. Professional opinions can differ widely about definitions, etiologies, and treatments. In short, psychiatry is still as much an art as it is a science. If the professionals cannot agree, where does this leave the employer who is aware that troubled senior executives are a problem and is sincerely motivated to help?

I define a mentally healthy individual as a person who is optimistic about the future, self-reliant yet able to delegate, organized and systematic, willing to accept authority but with a healthy degree of skepticism, competitive and assertive yet able to collaborate and compromise, able to gain satisfaction from a variety of sources, able to tolerate and ventilate strong emotions appropriately, open to intimacy yet able to set limits, flexible in the face of challenges, realistic about his or her strengths and weaknesses, able to advance his or her own welfare without exploiting others, hardworking but able to relax and enjoy leisure activities, and active and productive even under stress.

11

Cost of Executive Distress

How much are troubled senior executives costing their organizations? No one knows for sure. Although the costs of mental illness in the population as a whole and in the hourly employee work force in particular are generally well documented, data about the costs of troubled senior executives are not available. Many corporations do not keep separate records about the nature or cost to the firm of their impaired senior executives, preferring to merge these data with those for overall employee impairment. As a consequence, it is difficult to be precise in determining the costs of senior executive alcoholism, drug abuse, or mental illness within an organization. In addition, many of the costs of senior executive impairment are not quantifiable and, therefore, cannot be subjected to rigorous analysis.

Although difficult to measure, the costs of troubled senior executives fall into several categories. First is the cost of lost productivity, that is, paying substantial salary and benefits to a troubled senior executive who is not performing. An executive whose yearly salary is $400,000 and who receives an additional $100,000 a year in benefits but who works at only one-fifth of his or her maximum productive effort loses the firm more than $7,000 a week—a good deal more than the cost of the most expensive psychiatric treatment.

The second category of costs includes sick leave, absenteeism, health care costs, and disability payments. Troubled senior executives may be absent from the office for significant periods of time due to illness. If their illness has progressed to the point of no return, they may become permanently disabled and need to prematurely retire. Troubled senior executives may run up large health care bills, for example, for repeated hospitalizations for alcoholic cirrhosis of the liver, repeated psychiatric hospitalizations for recurrent depressive or psychotic episodes, and the like.

Termination and replacement costs make up the third category. The cost of replacing senior executives who must eventually be released can be quite high when the costs of recruitment, hiring, orientation, and training are included.

The fourth category includes the costs of poor professional judgment and bad business decisions. As noted earlier, troubled senior executives often display poor business judgment and make bad decisions that may adversely affect the firm as a whole—the more senior the executive, the greater the impact of the bad decision.

The fifth category includes the costs of lowered morale, negative publicity, and damage to the corporate image if the inappropriate actions and behaviors of troubled senior executives become public knowledge or widely known in the corporate community. Alcoholic executives embezzling corporate funds, manic executives getting involved in messy extramarital affairs, drug-dependent executives selling inside information to support their habit, depressed executives committing suicide, psychotic executives physically attacking other executives or employees—all are examples that fall within this fifth category.

Last of all are the costs of litigation when the organization has to defend itself against legal action taken by the terminated executive for wrongful discharge or discrimination. Legal action can also be initiated by other executives who may have been emotionally abused or physically harmed by the troubled executive.

Causes of Alcoholism, Drug Abuse, and Mental Illness

Although the causes of a few mental disorders have been fairly well established, the causes of many others are still matters of considerable debate within the psychiatric community. Part of the difficulty is one specific "cause" for the development of a given psychiatric disorder (Waldinger, 1986) can rarely be isolated. Psychiatric causation is a multidimensional concept (Nicholi, 1988). Research has only begun to unravel the complex relationships of heredity and constitution, pre- and postnatal care, early childhood experiences, family dynamics, socioeconomic and occupational factors, physical illness and injury, and cultural factors in the causation of mental illness, including alcoholism and drug addiction (Vaillant, 1983; Kaplan and Sadock, 1985). The view that all psychiatric illness is due to the impact of early childhood trauma or the result of abnormal neurochemical events is incorrect. Many of the psychiatric disorders have not been conclusively located in a specific region of the brain (although the limbic system is becoming an increasingly good candidate), and in many cases no definitive cerebral damage has been found at the gross anatomical level. Although some abnormalities in brain structure and function at the neuronal level have been discovered, it has not been conclusively demonstrated that these abnormalities are in all cases the causes of psychiatric illness rather than just associated findings (Torrey, 1983).

The problem of causation in psychiatric illness is not dissimilar to the situation in other branches of medicine, where causation of many illnesses is still not understood. In addition, individuals experience the factors of causation differently. Some may be greatly impacted by occupational stress, while others may be more affected by current family conflict. For some, childhood experiences will be the predominant factor, while for others heredity and constitution will play a crucial role. Also, different factors of causation will be more or less important during different periods of an individual's life (Waldinger, 1986). For example, occupational stress may be important in the causation of psychiatric illness for people in their twenties and thirties, but for older people the experience of the loss of loved ones—parents, older relatives, and so on—may begin to play a more important role. Further, many psychiatric patients are afflicted with several different disorders, including alcoholism and drug abuse, simultaneously, which makes for a very confusing picture of causation (Mirin, 1984). Because of the lack of agreement within the psychiatric community, there are currently a number of competing and overlapping schools of thought regarding the causes of mental illness (Kaplan and Sadock, 1985). For example, some theorists emphasize genetics and heredity, while others focus on early childhood trauma and disordered family interactions. Still others point to the importance of stress, socioeconomic, and sociocultural factors in the causation of mental illness. Another school of thought believes brain injury, trauma, and physical illness play an important role in the causation of mental illness.

Who is right? In a sense they all are. The human mind has both biological and psychological dimensions that interact in complex ways. The factors that contribute to the development of mental illness fall into two major groups, each having biological and psychological dimensions that interact and overlap complexly (Nicholi, 1988). The predisposing factors make up the first group and are defined as individual vulnerabilities of a biological or psychological nature (Kaplan and Sadock, 1985). Genetics, early childhood trauma, family dynamics, socioeconomic and sociocultural factors, and the aging process are in this group. The second group includes the precipitating factors—events or circumstances occurring immediately prior to the onset of the mental disorder that impact on the biological or psychological dimensions of the human mind and can be said to contribute to the appearance of the illness (Kaplan and Sadock, 1985). These factors include substance abuse and dependency, change in marital status, occupational stress, physical injury, illness, pregnancy, interpersonal conflict, family discord, financial strains, legal difficulties, and loss of a loved one.

Although in theory predisposing factors are clearly differentiated from precipitating factors, in reality the differences are not so apparent. In a given patient, it may be quite difficult to determine which factors are precipitating and which predisposing. For example, in addition to being psychiatric illnesses in their own right, substance abuse and dependency can be precipitating factors in the causation of other mental illnesses, such as acute psychosis and depression (Vaillant, 1983; Mirin, 1984). They can also be predisposing factors in the development of a number of organic mental disorders, including dementia, amnestic syndrome, organic delusional syndrome, organic hallucinosis, organic affective syndrome, and organic personality syndrome (Nicholi, 1988).

Alcoholism and drug abuse and dependency are psychiatric disorders in their own right (Vaillant, 1983; Mirin, 1984). The causes of alcoholism in executives and other individuals are still not clearly understood. One popular theory is that the causation of alcoholism is a function of genetic endowment. Family studies clearly show that relatives of alcoholics have a higher rate of alcoholism than the population as a whole (Kaplan and Sadock, 1985). Adoption studies conducted in Denmark concluded that adopted males whose biological parents were alcoholics were more than four times as likely to become alcoholics as adopted males whose parents were not alcoholics (Kaplan and Sadock, 1985). They usually developed severe cases of alcoholism by their early twenties and usually required treatment. Another theory of etiology is that alcoholism is a function of early childhood experience and family dynamics. Investigators have discovered that family histories of alcoholics often reveal childhood environments of marital and family conflict and parental emotional neglect. The child of an alcoholic is unable to get his or her emotional needs fulfilled and experiences feelings of anger, depression, and guilt. This emotional deprivation often leads to poor superego formation, with development of an overly rigid, punitive, and inadequate superego. There may also be poor ego formation characterized by poor impulse control, poor modification of aggressive instincts, and deficient self-control. Extended alcohol abuse also further impairs both ego and superego controls while diminishing the experience of anxiety. This increases the probability of further alcohol consumption. It is important to note that although both alcohol and drug use significantly distort psychological structures and functioning, many of these structures can recover dramatically during an extended period of sobriety with appropriate treatment. Many recovering substance abusers report improvements in self-esteem, better impulse control, and a decrease in guilt and self-punitive behavior.

A third theory of causation is that alcohol acts as a direct toxin on the brain, destroying vital brain tissue and significantly altering brain function. This results in the appearance of a variety of other psychiatric illnesses, including several of the organic mental disorders. There also appears to be a strong relationship between depression and the extended use of drugs or alcohol. Individuals who were depressed prior to drug or alcohol abuse frequently turn to drugs or alcohol as a way to ease their emotional pain. Unfortunately, continued use usually results in greater levels of depression rather than less because of the toxic effect of the substances on the brain. The deepening depression in turn results in continued alcohol or drug use, and the vicious cycle continues. It is also possible that depression shares the same genetic roots and biochemical pathways as drug and alcohol use; in other words, depression and alcohol and drug use may simply be different facets of the same biological disorder in the brain. The early childhood experiences of both depressed and substance-abusing persons appear to have similarities, suggesting yet another way in which these disorders may be related. When the above theories of etiology of alcoholism are viewed as a whole, a number of risk factors begin to emerge. These include (1) a family history of alcoholism; (2) sex—more men than women have problems with drinking; (3) age—men develop problems with alcohol in their twenties and thirties while women develop drinking problems later; (4) childhood history suggestive of psychological disturbance, including an attention deficit disorder or conduct disorder; and (5) other factors, including geography, occupation, racial background, nationality, income, and religion (Kaplan and Sadock, 1985).

What about the causes of drug abuse? Because there are so many different types of drugs to abuse and become dependent on, it is difficult to postulate one comprehensive theory of causation of drug abuse and dependency (Vaillant, 1983; Mirin, 1984). Also, as with alcohol, there is little agreement within the psychiatric community as to the definitive origins of drug abuse and dependency. Research data suggest that drug abuse and dependency are a disease caused by a complex interaction of biological vulnerabilities, psychological issues, and environmental settings. Drug abusers usually have a history of experimentation with more socially approved substances like tobacco, alcohol, and marijuana (Kaplan and Sadock, 1985). Recent studies also indicate that drug abusers have problems with poor impulse control, ego deficits, and an inability to appropriately manage intense affects, including anger and rage (Kaplan and Sadock, 1985). It is thought that some of these deficits in psychological structures and their associated functioning are in part a consequence rather than a cause of long-term chronic drug use. Becoming a drug abuser appears to be a function of the following: the cost, availability, and status of the drug; the financial condition of the drug abuser; the methods of initiation and the social supports that encourage continued usage; the psychological makeup and biological vulnerabilities of the individual; the type and intensity of current life stressors; the coping skills of the drug abuser; and the unwitting encouragement of the social or occupational environment. Drug abusers often have a low frustration tolerance and a need for immediate gratification. They are motivated to seek to induce and perpetuate a highly pleasurable mental state. Recent research indicates that certain drugs may impact on the genetically vulnerable brain to produce biochemical changes that further induce the drug-seeking and drug-taking behavior (Kaplan and Sadock, 1985).

Alcoholism and drug abuse can precipitate other psychiatric disorders in individuals via both psychological and biological mechanisms. Biologically speaking, substance abuse and addiction significantly impair brain functioning, resulting in problems with attention span, memory, concentration, and judgment. Psychologically speaking, substance abuse can be responsible for increased conflict with peers, friends, and family. Alcohol and drugs lessen impulse control and decrease adaptive abilities, frustration tolerance, and reliability. Alcohol and drug abuse can also precipitate mental and physical illnesses, including depression, psychosis, liver disease, gastrointestinal disease, and neurological illness.

What about the relationship between stress and the psychiatric disorders? In the 1930s Hans Selye was one of the first to define a stressor as an external stimulus that acts on the organism to produce a state of disequilibrium, or "stress" (Kaplan and Sadock, 1985). Further research uncovered general, unspecific responses of the body to a physical stressor, including changes in secretions of bodily chemicals such as catecholamines, endorphins, corticosteroids, and insulin. Selye pointed out in his later writings that stress can be either good or bad and that psychological events can have the same effect as physical stressors in producing the stress response (Kaplan and Sadock, 1985). More recently, stress has come to be defined as being the gap between the demands made on the individual and the individual's ability to cope with those demands. Too much stress can produce functional and structural damage, resulting in poor physical and mental health with impaired occupational and social functioning. Although the thesis that stress plays a major role in the precipitation of psychiatric illness is an attractive one, in recent years there has been disagreement about exactly what constitutes a stressful experience and about the exact mechanism by which stress exerts its effects as a precipitant. In the literature a "stressor" is considered to be an upsetting or potentially upsetting internal or external experience or event that might act as a trigger for the stress response. For example, a stressor can be physical, psychological, social, or existential. However, two individuals may experience the exact same "stressors" completely differently—one may become ill while the other remains completely unaffected. An individual's reaction to a specific stressor is affected by a number of factors, including genetic endowment, nervous system's readiness and ability to process stimulation, previous patterns of learned responses used to modify the experience of stress, and availability of psychosocial supports. Those individuals who have difficulty handling stress have a number of characteristics in common, including unrealistically high personal standards for performance; social isolation; low self-esteem and poor self-image; a hypercompetitive posture toward the world; a harsh, rigid, and punitive superego; and a low frustration tolerance. Individuals who develop depression usually have a history of prior stressful life events, including marriage, birth, death in the family, loss of job, and so forth, that appear to act as triggers in the development of their depression (Kaplan and Sadock, 1985). Stress management consultants recommend a variety of activities to increase coping skills. These include changing one's perceptions of the world, recognizing and accepting one's shortcomings, developing a sense of humor, setting realistic goals, conserving resources, managing time effectively, involving oneself socially, developing one's potential and self-reliance, balancing one's efforts between play and work, and scheduling effectively and planning in advance.

Working in the world is a demanding, challenging, stressful, and sometimes hazardous activity. Unfortunately, little hard research data are available to shed light on this important precipitating factor. My clinical experience with many employees and managers indicates that work can adversely affect one's psychological balance. Boring, unstimulating work in unpleasant and unattractive surroundings can contribute to the appearance of psychological distress. At the other extreme, individuals who experience work overload, or "burnout," frequently complain of a variety of somatic and psychological symptoms. Some workers may become emotionally distressed when they find themselves in a work situation for which they feel unqualified. Conflicts with superiors over unclear expectations, performance evaluation, or inconsistent or insufficient guidance and support can increase the level of psychologcial distress. Working environments that do not afford opportunities for developing a sense of accomplishment, personal growth, creative expression, and personal initiative can retard the development of high self-esteem and positive self-image. Major and unexpected changes in responsibilities can also contribute to anxiety and psychological distress. Such events include promotion or demotion, transfer to another location, retirement, and termination. Specific events such as mergers, acquisitions, and divestitures can also contribute to increased levels of emotional distress. Not all individuals experience events in the work place as emotionally distressing, nor will difficulties in the work place be the only contributing factor in the development of mental illness. Those individuals who by reason of their genetic endowment, early childhood experiences, and past medical and psychiatric history are predisposed to the development of psychiatric illness may have particular difficulty with the changing demands of the work place.

In spite of the fact that the causation of serious mental illness continues to generate controversy within the psychiatric community, there are a number of conclusions that can be drawn about the causes of psychiatric disorders. First, the factors responsible for mental illness in the affected senior executive are no different from the factors of causation of psychiatric disorders in other individuals. Second, psychiatric illness in executives and nonexecutives alike is the result of a complex interaction of predisposing and precipitating factors, including genetic endowment, early childhood experiences, aging, life stressors, occupational circumstances, socioeconomic and socio-cultural factors, physical illness and injury, interpersonal conflicts, family discord, financial and legal difficulties, and loss of a loved one. Third, there is and will continue to be a great deal of controversy within the psychiatric community as to the true causation of many of today's psychiatric disorders, whether they occur in executives or in others. Fourth, given the above conditions, it is very difficult to determine with certainty, much less predict in the individual senior executive's case, what combination of factors is truly responsible for the downfall. Fifth, the daily stress and strain of a demanding and challenging senior executive position is usually not the exclusive or the most important factor in the development of serious psychiatric illness in executives. Instead, the stress of a corporate position is just one of several nonspecific stressors that may contribute to the development of psychiatric illness in senior executives. Sixth, in senior executives and in others distorted psychological structures and impaired psychological functioning can both cause and be a result of long-term chemical abuse and dependency. Last of all, many psychiatrically impaired individuals have more than one mental disorder, which makes the determination of causation very difficult.

Summary

In this section I have briefly discussed what mental health and mental illness are; what troubled senior executives cost their organizations; and the causes of alcoholism, drug abuse, and mental illness. The following five chapters will introduce a number of seriously disturbed senior executives, whose histories will be used to show how to recognize their most common mental disturbances.

3

$\approx\!\approx$

In the Grip of the Bottle:
The Story of
an Alcoholic Executive

I first met Al while he was lying passed out on an emergency-room stretcher. He had just been admitted in a semicomatose state with a life-threatening blood-alcohol level, major gastrointestinal bleeding, and liver-function test results that were sky-high. Earlier that day he had imbibed, by his own account, at least a gallon of high-grade alcohol and several six-packs of beer. Al was a fifty-four-year-old senior executive and father of two grown children, ages twenty-one and twenty-three. For the past fifteen years he had been a very successful senior vice-president for marketing for a high-technology firm. For several weeks prior to his admission to the emergency room, Al had greatly increased his drinking. Things were not going well for him at the office, and he began to attempt to drown his sorrows every night after work with larger and larger amounts of vodka, wine, and beer. The night of his admission, his wife had come home after an evening shopping trip to find Al passed out on the floor of the bathroom adjacent to the master bedroom. She became alarmed when she was unable to revive him and called the ambulance that brought him to the hospital.

What happened to Al? Why did he go off the deep end when he appeared to have so much going for him? What was his problem? Al was an alcoholic. For many people the term brings to mind images of skid-row derelicts sipping cheap wine out of brown paper bags in the back alleys of our major cities. As Al's story clearly demonstrates, however, alcoholism is a disease that can also destroy the lives and careers of highly successful businesspersons and professionals. One survey discovered that 35 percent of the 635 members of an Alcoholics Anonymous chapter were managers or professionals (Stimmel, 1984). Thirty percent of all practicing lawyers have been found to have abused alcohol (Frances, 1984), while more than 224,000 physicians drink regularly, and 22,600 doctors, 9,000 dentists, and 75,000 nurses are alcoholics (Busch, 1982; Bissell and Jones, 1981). Like all alcoholics, senior executives with a serious drinking problem can exhibit a wide range of difficulties with alcohol:

> The sixty-eight-year-old CEO of a small family-owned retail establishment who drank two fifths of alcohol a day for forty years began having significant memory lapses and started to experience hallucinations. His thinking and behavior became so disturbed that he was no longer able to lead and assume initiative. He had to be removed from office.

> A senior manager with a long history of alcohol abuse had too much to drink and went on a binge, assaulted his wife, and was charged by the police.

> A middle-aged, divorced woman and senior vice-president for marketing who abused vodka became depressed on the weekend and overdosed on alcohol and sleeping pills.

> A partner in a major accounting firm with a history of four driving-while-intoxicated convictions had too much to drink one evening at a company social function and slammed his car into a tree at eighty miles an hour.

> The chairman of the board collapsed in his office just before an important meeting of the board, vomiting blood from ulcers developed from thirty-five years of drinking.

The middle-aged senior executive of the telephone company with a severe alcohol problem was admitted four times in five years to alcohol-rehabilitation programs. Total costs for the treatments and the lost productivity exceeded several hundred thousand dollars. The senior executive was finally retired on medical disability at the age of forty-nine.

An alcoholic is anyone who engages in repeated, excessive, uncontrolled drinking of alcoholic beverages that leads to significant impairment of physical health and occupational and social functioning. Individuals who are dependent on or addicted to alcohol experience withdrawal symptoms after a reduction or cessation of drinking. In many ways senior executives are no different than other alcoholics, but the consequences of alcoholism in senior executives may be far greater than the consequences of alcoholism in an hourly employee. Alcoholic senior executives may forget crucial meetings or deadlines. They may become suspicious and distrustful and may alienate important clients or business partners. They may lose their political savvy and derail an important business deal. They may become indecisive and confused and not be able to make an important business decision. They may lose all sense of perspective, misinterpret events in their business environment, and commit the firm to a disastrous course of action.

History of Al's Drinking Problem

Although frightening, Al's case is, unfortunately, in no way unusual or remarkable, and Al was no derelict. The oldest of six children, Al grew up in modest circumstances in an Irish Catholic household in south Boston. His father, Bill, was a rough-and-tumble Irishman who grew up on the streets of south Boston and came from a long line of "two-fisted drinkers." Al's grandmother, who lived with the family during Al's childhood, was a quiet drinker who was known to enjoy her brandy. Now in her late eighties, she had become demented—a condition resulting from fifty years of drinking. At the age of forty-three Al's grandfather died from a ruptured blood vessel and cirrhosis of the liver. In high school, Al and several of his classmates occasionally went out on Friday nights to have a few beers that were purchased with the help of some fake identification. In college he continued to put his social life ahead of academics. He gained a reputation for being able to down a couple of six-packs on a weekday night and still be able to attend classes the next day. After college Al decided to go into sales, a field that he thought would suit him well, and he was right. He became an immediate success. He married his high school sweetheart after graduation and began his career working for a small electronics firm in Boston. He worked there for a number of years, until he received the offer from his current boss.

Al specialized in the marketing of a broad line of personal and minicomputer systems for small businesses and departments of large companies. Every year for the past fifteen years, sales of his product line had exceeded expectations. Before his hospitalization Al was well on his way to turning in the best year of his career, despite his drinking.

In spite of his professional success, Al gradually became a "prisoner of the bottle." As he tells it:

> I mostly remember being drunk most of the time. I had a tough job. Although I was very good at sales, it took a lot out of me. I guess I didn't realize what the wear and tear of the constant travel and entertainment were doing to me. I was away from the office at least two to three days out of every week. I guess I drank like a fish in order to ease the pressures of being on the road and to cut the boredom.

Al enjoyed staying at good hotels and eating and drinking well, and he liked to conduct business over an expensive lunch or dinner. He said that it would not be unusual for him to have three or four cocktails before dinner, a bottle and a half of wine with the meal, and a couple of cordials after the meal. Al felt that the alcohol helped make him a less anxious and more effective communicator. He also felt that it helped make the potential client more receptive to his presentation.

I was drinking all the time. I kept several flasks of liquor in my overnight bag, and I sipped from them on the plane, in the airport, and during the long taxi rides into town. In the mornings my hands would shake so badly that I couldn't shave until I had several drinks to settle my nerves. Even fellow sales reps who sometimes traveled with me, and who were no teetotalers themselves, started to tell me that I was slurring my words and smelling of alcohol throughout the day. In the evenings after returning to the hotel suite following a reception I would sometimes stumble over the furniture just walking to the bathroom.

About two months before his admission Al tried to stop by abruptly "going on the wagon," which turned out to be a big mistake. Six days after Al stopped drinking, he began to feel strange. He began to sweat and feel nauseous, and his friends commented that he looked pale and tired.

I woke up abruptly one night and thought I saw hundreds of black spiders crawling up the walls and overrunning the place. I threw one of the bedroom lamps at the wall in a futile attempt to kill some of the spiders. I thought my bedroom was a hotel suite and I thought my wife was the hotel manager. I kept demanding that my wife fumigate the room immediately. I then ran down the stairs, out the front door, and into the street, still in my nightclothes. My wife called the police, and a short time later I was picked up several blocks from my home. I was taken to a local hospital to "dry out," and I was released twenty-eight days later.

The Disease of Alcoholism

In many ways Al's story is typical of the experience of many who have the disease of alcoholism. Alcoholics experience a slow, chronic, downhill course extending over many years with high levels of denial that they have a drinking problem and with increasingly brief periods of sobriety. Alcoholism was officially recognized as a disease by the American Medical Association in 1956 and by the American Hospital Association and the AFL-CIO in 1957 and 1959, respectively. Alcoholism is not simply a defect of character or a "moral weakness." Alcohol is a potent chemical that has a major impact on the brain and other organs. The active ingredient in most spirits is ethyl alcohol. Twenty percent of alcohol that is ingested is absorbed into the bloodstream from the stomach, and 80 percent is absorbed from the small intestine. Alcohol is absorbed quickly and can be measured in the blood within five minutes of ingestion; the peak concentration occurs after one-half to two hours. Milk and other fatty foods impede the absorption of alcohol, and water significantly enhances it. Alcohol acts as a depressant on the central nervous system and significantly impairs motor performance and all new learning. Alcoholism is a factor in a wide range of illnesses, including nutritional diseases (undernutrition, malnutrition, vitamin deficiencies), neurological disorders (brain damage, dementia, Wernicke's syndrome, Korsakoff's psychosis, peripheral neuropathy), disorders of the heart (cardiomyopathy), disorders of the gastrointestinal system (poor absorption, gastritis, duodenal ulcers, esophagitis, pancreatitis, cirrhosis of the liver, alcoholic hepatitis), disorders of the muscles (skeletal myopathies), disorders of the endocrine system, disorders of the blood system (anemia), and disorders of the immune system. About 10 percent of alcoholics develop cirrhosis of the liver as well as the associated esophageal varices, liver failure, and liver cancer. Alcoholics also have a high incidence of cancer of the mouth, throat, esophagus, and stomach.

Alcoholics, like Al, share a number of salient characteristics and behaviors. These include the need for alcohol on a daily basis in order to function adequately ("I was always looking for the next drink—I couldn't face the day at work without a couple of shots in the morning"); the inability to decrease or stop drinking for an extended period of time ("I thought I could control it but I couldn't—it controlled me"); the desire to remain continually intoxicated for several days or longer; the consumption of a fifth or more of spirits a day; the combining of alcohol with other drugs; the experiencing of blackouts ("There were days at a time that I just couldn't remember what happened"); the ignoring of major medical or neurological illnesses that are the result of or exacerbated by continued drinking ("I got stomach ulcers from my drinking but didn't care if I bled to death—I just needed the next drink"); poor social and occupational functioning, including absences from the job, poor job performance, arguments with superiors and peers, and poor marital relations; and legal difficulties resulting from driving while intoxicated ("I was dragged into court more than once for driving while intoxicated. I was a real menace on the road. I drove like a maniac. I would always make sure that I had a case of booze in the back of the car in case I found myself without a liquor store nearby.").

When alcoholics adjust to chronically high blood levels of alcohol, the result is development of a tolerance in the central nervous system. Al gradually increased the amount of alcohol that he consumed, so that by the time he started treatment he had been drinking very large amounts on a daily basis—before, during, and after work. He developed such a tolerance for alcohol that he had to drink larger and larger amounts to get the same effect. Alcoholics, like Al, who abruptly stop drinking often experience withdrawal symptoms. The signs and symptoms of the alcohol withdrawal syndrome include tremors, nausea, vomiting, fatigue, increased heartbeat, profuse sweating, elevated blood pressure, anxiety, depression, sleep difficulties, grand mal seizures, headache, nightmares, and disordered sense perceptions. Al developed the "morning shakes"—a characteristic of the withdrawal syndrome that results from the temporary decrease in his blood-alcohol level during sleep.

The signs and symptoms of delirium tremens include many of the signs of alcohol withdrawal with the addition of significant confusion, poor concentration, shortened attention span, disorientation, impaired memory, poor insight and judgment, agitation, delusions, and auditory and visual hallucinations. Al became physically dependent on the alcohol to the point that when he abruptly stopped drinking on his own, he soon went

into withdrawal. Delirium tremens is a very serious condition—
15 percent of alcoholics in the throes of delirium tremens die
due to increased body temperature or acute collapse of the general circulation.

Myths of Executive Alcoholism

Recognizing the early symptoms of Al's drinking problem would
have been a crucial step in getting him the proper treatment for
his drinking problem. But before employers can learn how to
detect the early warning signs of alcohol abuse and addiction,
they must first confront certain myths and misunderstandings
about executive alcoholism that can become significant barriers
to effective early detection and treatment of the alcoholic senior executive.

*Myth Number One   Alcohol abuse in senior executives is
not a disease but simply a lack of willpower—a kind of moral
weakness. Any senior executive can "overcome" the drinking
problem if he or she really has the desire to do so.* Unfortunately, this is not the case. The central premise of the disease
concept of alcohol is that the alcoholic cannot control his or her
drinking—one drink usually leads, in time, to twenty. Alcoholism is a chronic, long-term disease over which one has no control and which has an inevitable downhill course. There is no
cure except to stop drinking—completely and for good. There
are only recovering alcoholics—not recovered alcoholics. Alcoholics who have not touched a drop of alcohol in twenty-five
years are still vulnerable if they take even one drink. An alcoholic can no more control his or her drinking than a diabetic
can control the malfunctioning of the pancreas. There are very
few if any successful "social drinkers" among alcohol abusers
and addicts. As a consequence, hoping that the alcoholic senior
executive, with a little encouragement, will be able to "cut
back" and return to the ranks of the social drinkers is wrong.
An alcoholic's inability to successfully cut back his or her drinking is not evidence of "moral weakness" or a general "lack of

willpower." There are a number of senior executives who are aggressive, assertive, and disciplined in their jobs but who are not able to control their drinking.

Myth Number Two *Alcoholic senior executives, once confronted, will be forthcoming, open, and candid about their alcohol use.* Alcoholics, whether executives or others, are notorious for talking themselves and others into believing that they do not have a problem. They are great rationalizers and deceivers—deceiving both themselves and others about the seriousness of their drinking problem. They will often go so far as to hide empty bottles and to drink only in secret. In addition, many of the alcoholic's friends, colleagues, and family members simply prefer not to see the truth. Denial can be particularly strong in those corporate environments in which alcohol consumption is considered a routine and accepted part of the way the firm does business. This head-in-the-sand approach to drinking problems is certainly not helpful in the short run and is disastrous in the long run. A corporate or family attitude of denial enables the alcoholic senior executive to continue her or his disastrous course. Senior executives with major alcohol problems can be found in virtually every industry and every region of the country. Even companies that ban the use of alcohol on the premises discover to their dismay that they have senior executives who abuse or are addicted to alcohol. Denial is a particularly large problem in those firms in which the chairman of the board, the CEO, or one or more members of the senior management team has a significant drinking problem that they deny. Denial at the top sets the tone all the way down the line. A good way to test the level of one's own denial is to ask oneself if one suspects or has suspected at least one senior executive in one's firm of having or recovering from a drinking problem. If the answer to this question is no, then one's level of denial or lack of awareness may be too high.

Myth Number Three *Off-hours alcohol use and abuse do not necessarily affect the senior executive's productivity and performance on the job.* Not true. Significant alcohol abuse, even if it is during one's "off hours," still affects one's ability to perform optimally in a large number of ways, including (1) the lingering chronic toxic effects of alcohol on the brain, interfering with sound business judgment, memory, insight, orientation, and mood and producing unpredictable consequences on behavior; (2) the sapping of energy and initiative throughout the day; (3) the constant preoccupation with the next drink, distracting one from the work at hand; (4) the nonproductive periods of acute intoxication or recovery from binges and hangovers lasting for days; and (5) the medical complications of alcohol abuse, including ulcers, cirrhosis of the liver, pneumonia, malnutrition, and cancer, resulting in medical evaluations, treatments, and hospitalizations with subsequent time lost at work.

Al was the victim of alcoholism. From a neurophysiological point of view, alcohol acted as a toxin that altered and distorted his brain structure and function. From a genetic point of view, Al was the product of a family that had significant problems with alcohol—his father, grandmother, and grandfather were heavy drinkers and possibly abusers of alcohol. Given this family history, it is likely that Al was genetically at risk of inheriting a biochemical vulnerability to alcoholism. The strong family tradition of drinking undoubtedly shaped Al's early views about drinking as a highly desirable social activity. During the course of his recovery, he admitted that he equated heavy drinking with manhood and believed that it was a socially approved way of doing business. He firmly believed that alcohol facilitated his social interaction and made him a better executive. Al's early psychological development was probably adversely influenced by his father's alcohol problems and the history of marital conflict.

Results of psychological testing administered during Al's hospitalization provided further evidence of his impaired psychological development. The test results indicated that Al was a depressed and angry individual with very low self-esteem and a poor self-image, which he attempted to boost by succeeding in the traditional way in his chosen field of endeavor. The results further indicated that Al had problems with poor impulse control, reacted defensively to criticism, adapted poorly to

changing environmental circumstances, had difficulty with intimate relationships, and used primarily denial, repression, and
projection—he used drinking to defend against intrapsychic pain.
Poor psychological functioning caused Al to continue to drink,
which in turn caused greater impairment in his psychological
functioning. Al's various psychological impairments were also
apparent during the initial phase of his hospitalization in both
group and individual therapy. Al had great difficulty opening up
and relating in more than a superficial way to other patients and
staff on the unit. He used a gregarious, joking, and confident demeanor to hide his personal insecurities. He reacted defensively
to constructive criticism and had a low frustration tolerance,
with difficulty accepting the rules and limits of the unit. At
times he would sulk and appear moody and would refuse to talk
to the other patients and staff about what was really bothering
him. He had difficulty identifying and expressing his emotions
and resisted developing insight into the reasons for his current
difficulties with alcohol.

    After a period of time in the hospital, Al began to open
up more. In his counseling sessions he described himself as an
angry and depressed individual who frequently felt disappointed
in his father, whom he loved, feared, and resented. Al felt that
as a child he never got enough attention or guidance from his
father. Al learned to suppress his anger, resentment, and depression and instead tried to be like his father, using alcohol to
drown his emotional pain. He believed that his habit of caring
for long-term clients like they were part of the family was a result of his childhood sense of deficient parenting—if he could
not have his father's love and attention, then at least he could
be like a father to others. What role did Al's stressful work environment play in the development of his alcoholism? The long
hours, frequent travel, erratic eating patterns, conflicts with his
peers and boss, and high expectations for performance were job
stressors that contributed to Al's alcohol problems.

    In sum, Al was predisposed to the development of alco-
holism due to genetic endowment and emotional deprivation in
childhood, with deficient psychological development and early
exposure to family and cultural role models. Al's alcoholic pre-

disposition gradually evolved into an acute alcohol problem be-cause of a number of precipitating factors, including the long-term biological and psychological effects of continued alcohol use; the continuing impact of deficient psychological structures and associated psychological conflicts; the social, occupational, and cultural reinforcers for alcohol abuse; and the presence of occupational stress and interpersonal conflict.

Recognizing the Alcoholic Executive

What are the symptoms of alcoholism? There are four groups of symptoms. The first category includes inappropriate attitudes about alcohol and unusual patterns of alcohol consumption. Pay attention to senior executives who reach for a drink as a re-lief from stress and who, like Al, see the consumption of large quantities of alcohol as a necessary part of doing business. Watch out for senior executives who at social functions gulp three or four drinks quickly to "loosen up." Notice those senior executives who seem to have a compulsion to drink more than others and who disparage nondrinkers in the group.

The second group of symptoms includes changes in pro-fessional behavior, work performance, work routines, and pro-ductivity. Alcoholics will often become irascible, irritable, diffi-cult to get along with, temperamental, erratic, and defensive about their excessive drinking. Personality changes are due to the direct acute and chronic toxic effects of alcohol on the brain. Quiet senior executives will become blowhards. Extrovert senior executives will become withdrawn and isolated. Alcoholic senior executives will lose their interpersonal skills, and other executives in the office will begin to complain about how diffi-cult it is to work with them.

Note a falloff in the quality and quantity of a senior executive's work—missed deadlines, chronic lateness with im-portant projects, sloppy work, and poor presentations. Pay at-tention to the formerly sharp senior executive who develops poor business judgment and begins to make bad business deci-sions. Pay attention to senior executives who are away from the office on Mondays and Fridays, take frequent medical leaves of several days' duration, and are unaccounted for during the middle of the workday. Alcoholics miss work due to alcoholic binges, recovering from a hangover, or recuperating from a medical illness related to alcohol use.

The third group of symptoms of alcoholism consists of the physical signs of alcohol abuse and addiction. Watch for the smell of alcohol on the breath, particularly in the early morning when the senior executive comes to work. This indicates that he or she has had a couple of drinks before coming to the office—most likely to calm the "morning shakes." "Morning shakes" are tremors of the hands in the morning that make it difficult to shave without cutting oneself or to hold a cup of coffee without spilling it. These tremors are due to lowered blood-alcohol levels during the eight hours of sleep, inducing a mild withdrawal reaction when the alcoholic arises. The morning shakes are a sign of a very serious alcohol problem.

Look for repeated episodes of medical illness, with hospitalizations, medical evaluations, extended treatments, and time lost from work. As noted earlier in the chapter, there are a large number of medical illnesses associated with acute and chronic alcohol abuse. Notice changes in the facial skin of the executive—an increasingly ruddy complexion with the appearance of very small blood vessels on the nose and face may indicate excessive alcohol use. Pay attention to a gradual increase in weight, gained mostly in the stomach and abdomen. Weight gain is due primarily to the high caloric content of some alcoholic beverages. In a small number of cases the weight will be due to the accumulation of fluid ascites in the abdominal cavity from advanced liver disease. Some alcoholics will experience a drop in weight, usually due to the restricted intake of a proper diet in favor of alcohol.

Be aware of the senior executive who sustains repeated injuries, including head injuries, broken ribs, or broken limbs due to "accidental falls." Poor judgment and loss of gross and fine motor coordination during intoxicated states can result in the alcoholic's losing his or her balance and falling, resulting in a variety of injuries. Be attuned to the senior executive who comes to the office in the morning looking "run-down" and fatigued, complaining of little energy or unable to concentrate, with a headache and reddened eyes, who drinks five to ten cups of coffee before he or she can begin to function. Alcoholics can engage in all-night "benders" in which they get little sleep due to their drinking. Alcohol is not conducive to a good night's sleep.

The fourth and last major group of symptoms of alcoholism is significant and repeated legal difficulties. Alcoholics come to the attention of the court for a variety of reasons, including drunkenness in public and creating a public disturbance, assault-and-battery charges for violent outbursts while in an acutely intoxicated state, and car accidents due to driving while under the influence of alcohol.

Summary

Al was the victim of the disease of alcoholism. His disease disrupted his friendships, impaired his professional performance, and threatened his career. There are four groups of early warning signs of senior executive alcoholism, including (1) inappropriate attitudes about alcohol and unusual patterns of alcohol consumption; (2) changes in professional behavior, personality, work performance, and overall productivity; (3) physical signs and symptoms of alcohol abuse and addiction; and (4) repeated legal difficulties. In later chapters I will turn to the challenge of getting a senior executive like Al into treatment, keeping him in treatment, and getting him integrated back into the firm after treatment.

4

~~~~~~

Getting High:
The Story of an
Executive Cocaine Abuser

My introduction to Victor and his cocaine problem came
from his father, Victor, Sr., the sixty-two-year-old chairman and
chief executive officer of a privately held, diversified manufacturing firm. Victor, Jr., the chief financial officer of the firm,
had just pleaded guilty to charges of illegally distributing and
transporting a pound of cocaine across state lines.

Victor's illegal drug involvement came as a complete surprise to his father:

> I don't understand it. He owns a twelve-room house and
> a large summer home, both of which were made possible
> by very large, below-market-rate loans I provided him
> through the firm. At the age of forty he's the youngest
> member of the senior executive group, and in a couple of
> years he could have looked forward to succeeding me as
> chairman and chief executive officer when I retire. He's
> married to a wonderful woman and has two lovely chil-
> dren. He's well thought of in the community, having been
> active in civic affairs and a generous contributor to a
> number of cultural and educational institutions in the
> city. My son has got everything anyone could ask for.
> Why did he do it?

36

Cocaine abuse and drug addiction are all around us. In 1983 cocaine was estimated to be a $26.8 to $32.2 billion per year industry (Masi, 1984). Nearly one in ten Americans and one in seven high school students have experimented with cocaine (Schuckit, 1986). The use of illicit drugs can be found in both sexes and in all races, ethnic groups, occupations, age groups, and regions of the country. Although drug abuse and drug addiction in executives, managers, and administrators are certainly not common, the available data strongly support the contention that illicit drug use is far from rare among the professional and managerial elite. In one study 26 percent of a group of drug abusers were found to hold significant professional or managerial jobs (Stimmel, 1984). A study of 114 business executives admitted to either of two hospitals during a two-year period discovered that the average business executive who abused drugs had been addicted for least two years, was thirty years of age, was white and male, and had an average income of $42,000 a year (Stimmel, 1984). In a survey of 136 cocaine abusers, 53 percent were in the top third of their social class (Helfrich, Crowley, Atkinson, and Post, 1982). In another survey of seventy cocaine abusers, the average family income was $83,000; 37 percent of the cocaine abusers in this group admitted to either stealing or dealing in order to support their habit, which at times cost them as much as $3,000 a week (Stimmel, 1984). The mean age of this group was thirty-one, and it included corporate executives, business owners, professionals, and salespersons. They averaged sixteen years of formal education, and 84 percent were white males who had been abusing cocaine for an average of four years (Stimmel, 1984).

Why did Victor do it? He was a cocaine abuser who, like many drug abusers, used the proceeds from his drug sales to finance an increasingly expensive habit. Cocaine abuse is part of a broader category of drug abuse that is defined as being the pathological use of chemical substances that results in significant impairment of occupational or social functioning. Drug-dependent individuals differ from drug abusers in that they not only exhibit pathological use of the drug but also become physi-

ologically dependent, develop tolerance, and experience withdrawal symptoms when they cease use of the substance. *Drug
addict* is a layman's term that generally refers to anyone who
abuses or is dependent on drugs. Senior executives like Victor
who become involved in illicit drug use experience a wide range
of difficulties:

> A forty-two-year-old Wall Street senior executive with a
> $2,000-a-day cocaine habit embezzled several hundred
> dollars from his investment banking firm to support his
> drug habit before he was caught.

> A thirty-eight-year-old senior vice-president of opera-
> tions for a West Coast firm who daily ingested large
> amounts of amphetamines to help him keep "alert and
> awake" during his sixteen-hour workday began to hear
> "voices," became paranoid, and physically threatened
> his boss.

> A fifty-two-year-old chief executive officer of a
> midwestern family-owned firm who took increasing
> amounts of prescribed painkillers for an old back injury
> became addicted to the medication and had to be
> admitted to a chemical-dependency treatment unit to
> be detoxified.

> A forty-two-year-old woman senior executive for a large
> New York advertising firm who took increasing amounts
> of a prescribed minor tranquilizer for "nerves and ten-
> sion" eventually overdosed on a combination of tran-
> quilizers and alcohol.

> A thirty-nine-year-old partner of a prestigious law
> firm who developed a $2,500-a-day cocaine habit was
> caught misappropriating funds from clients' escrow
> accounts.

Victor's History of Drug Abuse

Victor, Jr., was raised as an only child in comfortable upper-middle-class surroundings in upstate New York. Except for several distant uncles who were known to "drink heavily," his family was free from any problem with drugs, alcohol, or mental illness. Victor was never close to his father because of his long work hours. As a consequence, Victor spent a great deal of time in his mother's company. He was somewhat of a loner, a child who preferred staying at home playing by himself or going out with his mother. From the beginning he did very well in school. During his elementary school years his teachers noted that the work came very easily to him but that he had a very low frustration tolerance and would turn away from the occasional task that taxed his abilities. He often refused to play with other children during recess, preferring to read at his desk. At home when his mother said no to his frequent demands, Victor would hold his breath until he turned blue and threatened to pass out. His mother usually gave in.

In high school Victor was chubby, the product of his mother's good cooking. He felt awkward in most social settings, and he did not date or involve himself in extracurricular activities. During high school, "mostly out of boredom," Victor began smoking marijuana, which was readily available from student drug dealers and which he could afford with his substantial weekly allowance. He experimented only once with LSD because of a "bad trip," used amphetamines occasionally to stay up late to cram for an exam, and would imbibe one too many beers after the local high school football games. Victor smoked marijuana once or twice a week throughout his entire high school career with what appeared to be few ill effects. He graduated first in his high school class and elected to attend a college in upstate New York while living at home, even though he had been accepted by several Ivy League schools. The prospect of eating dormitory food and having to share a suite with several strangers was not an idea Victor found attractive. In addition, he figured that he would never be able to fit his Steinway into his dormitory suite.

Victor did well in college, concentrating in economics and graduating magna cum laude and Phi Beta Kappa in spite of continued weekly use of marijuana and alcohol. Although in his senior year he was accepted to several nationally known business schools, he decided to accept an entry-level position at a Wall Street investment banking firm with which he had worked for several summers during his college years. He was attracted to the excitement and glamor of Wall Street. He believed that Wall Street would broaden his horizons in ways upstate New York never could. He was right. It was at a fashionable party in Manhattan that Victor was first introduced to cocaine. He found it very much to his liking.

After two years at the investment banking firm, Victor decided to attend business school for his master's degree. He did well despite the demanding academic schedule and his continued use of marijuana, alcohol, and now cocaine. During his second year of studies, he met Jan, a woman in his class from a prominent New York family whose forebears had founded one of the major Wall Street investment banking firms. Victor, Sr., said that both he and Victor, Jr., were impressed by Jan's elegance, intelligence, and family background. Although Jan initially showed little interest in Victor, he pursued her relentlessly. In time she grew to like him in spite of his abrasive style and more humble origins. They were married the week after their graduation from business school. Victor was offered a position with his old firm at an increase in salary and was firmly on the fast track to partnership.

At the end of his first year at the investment banking firm, things appeared to get out of hand for Victor. He was under terrific pressure at the firm, no longer able to coast by on his intelligence alone. He worked very long hours—sometimes eighty, ninety, even a hundred hours a week. It was not uncommon for Victor to stay up all night working on a deal, then go home in the early morning for only a brief shower and a change of business suits before heading back to the office. In spite of the intense competition, after six difficult and draining years Victor made it—at the age of thirty he was one of the youngest individuals to make partner in the history of the firm. But by the end of his sixth year he was using cocaine daily. The increased frequency of his cocaine use convinced Victor that he had a serious drug problem. He talked his boss into giving him a four-week vacation. Unknown to anyone except his wife, Victor admitted himself to an out-of-state, twenty-eight-day drug-rehabilitation program. After the program he returned to work. He felt better than he had in years and was convinced that he had kicked the habit. Unfortunately, he was wrong. Soon after he was hired by his father, Victor, Sr., to be the chief financial officer for the family firm, Victor started using cocaine again. He was convinced that an occasional "line of coke" would not be a problem, but it was.

About a year after Victor, Sr., had hired his son, he began to worry about Victor.

I noticed that Victor didn't seem to be his usual self. I noticed that he seemed more depressed and withdrawn and generally had little to say. Some of his colleagues complained to me that Victor would often disappear from the office during the day for several hours at a time without telling anyone where he was. Other executives complained to me that he became easily irritated and was increasingly difficult to get along with. In meetings that I attended, Victor seemed to lose track of points. During the last month before his arrest, he started to complain to me in private that he believed that others in the corporation were out to do him in and trying to get him fired. I tried to assure him that this was not the case as far as I knew. I also noticed that he appeared to be losing weight; his clothes were ill fitting and appeared to hang on him. At one point I asked if he had been dieting, but he denied it.

When I would run into my son early in the mornings at the office he was constantly complaining of fatigue and headaches, and that he hadn't slept well the night before. He would state that he felt nauseous for much of the day. In fact, things seemed to be getting so bad that his wife, Jan, called me to find out what was

going on at the office. Victor would come home late
every evening in a terrible mood and would usually go
right to bed without dinner and without telling her why
he was upset. I told Jan that probably the pressures of
the new job were getting to Victor and suggested that
they take a short vacation without the kids to get away
from it all. They did manage to get away for about a
week, but on his return to work Victor appeared no
better.

Victor, Sr., went on to explain that during the last year
Victor, Jr., traveled to Miami several times a month but typically stayed no longer than a day each time. When Victor, Sr.,
asked his son about the trips, he simply said that he was con-
sidering investing in some real estate in the Miami area and needed
to make frequent trips to better assess the properties. Only after
Victor, Jr., was indicted, was arrested, and pleaded guilty to the
charges did his father realize that Victor, Jr., was interested in
more than real estate in Florida.

Nature of Cocaine and Drug Abuse

Today the most commonly abused drugs fall into a number of
categories, including stimulants; barbiturates, sedatives, and
hypnotics; opioids; hallucinogens; and cannabinoids. The stimulants (cocaine and the amphetamines), the minor tranquilizers
within the barbiturate class (Valium and Librium), and the cannabinoids (marijuana and hashish) are the drugs executives most
commonly abuse. Cocaine is a naturally occurring alkaloid that
is extracted from the leaf of the coca bush and is a powerful
stimulant of the central nervous system that results in a high degree of psychological rather than physical dependence. It is
either smoked, injected, or inhaled. After ingestion the drug
quickly reaches the brain and produces a short-lived but powerful euphoria associated with small pupils, elevated blood pressure, and increased rate of respiration and pulse. The feeling of
euphoria diminishes quickly, depending on the dose and the
route of administration. Cocaine gives the addict temporary feel-

ings of increased energy, grandiosity, assertiveness, self-esteem, exhilaration, increased self-confidence, and increased sexual interest. After the brief high of cocaine there is a letdown accompanied by feelings of depression, lassitude, and an intense craving for more of the drug. A desire to experience the intense high quickly becomes an obsession as the frequency and the dosage escalate. For some cocaine abusers daily needs for food and shelter take a backseat to the search for the drug. Largely because of its high price, cocaine is considered a highly desirable "elite" drug, particularly among certain professional and managerial classes under the age of forty-five. A new smokable form of cocaine, called rock or crack, has recently been introduced. This form, which is sometimes referred to as poor-man's cocaine, is made by mixing cocaine with baking soda and cooking it into a hardened substance that resembles small rocks in appearance. It is inexpensive and easy to make. It is also safer than other, purer forms of cocaine such as that produced by free-basing. In its smokable form cocaine reaches the brain in ten to twenty seconds and produces an intense high, quickly followed by a letdown. Crack is sold for as little as ten dollars a smoke, and cocaine dealers can gross thousands of dollars a week selling it on the street. Cocaine can kill a person in a number of ways, including fatal septicemia, hepatitis, respiratory depression, and cardiac problems.

Other drugs within the stimulant class include the amphetamines, such as benzedrine, dexedrine, and ritalin. Amphetamines are drugs that produce a sense of heightened energy, alertness, and euphoria. They are used in weight-reduction programs, to treat attention-deficit disorders in children, and to increase alertness. Students, executives, and busy professionals turn to them in times of high stress and rushed deadlines. Amphetamines can cause a high degree of psychological dependence but generally do not cause physical dependence or withdrawal symptoms. Nevertheless, the amphetamine "crash," or letdown after the use of the drug, can produce a very severe depression that may lead to suicidal ideation.

The barbiturates, sedatives, and hypnotics comprise the second class of abused drugs. Substances in this class include

Valium, Librium, Nembutal, Seconal, Tuinal, Doriden, Noludar, Placidyl, Miltown, and Equanil. On the street they are called reds, red devils, downers, yellow jackets, yellows, seggies, nembies, rainbows, double trouble, and tooies. Although the first barbiturate, barbitone, was introduced in 1903, the most commonly used barbiturates are prescription drugs that have been introduced during the past thirty years, including Valium and Librium, which are popular muscle relaxants and antianxiety agents. Many senior executives who abuse these chemicals receive them via prescription from their family physician to help relieve day-to-day anxieties, to help with muscle tension, or to relieve insomnia. Individuals can develop strong physical and psychological dependence on and increasing tolerance of drugs in this class, requiring larger and larger amounts, which are easily obtainable by "doctor shopping" for repeat prescriptions of the drugs. People who cease using these drugs abruptly may experience withdrawal symptoms.

The third class of abused drugs is the cannabinoids, which have sedative, stimulant, and some mild hallucinogenic properties. This class includes marijuana and hashish, which is derived from a sticky yellowish resin on the leaves and flowers of the hemp plant. There are several different grades of cannabinoids. The least potent grade, called bhang, has a very low resin content. This is the grade of much of the marijuana available in the United States. The middle grade is called ganhja, and it has a higher resin content. The highest grade is called charas and is known in the United States as hashish. Hashish is made from the resin itself and is five to eight times more potent than marijuana. The cannabinoids produce a dreamy state, with heightened sensitivity to external stimuli, distortion of sense of time, mood changes, and some distortions in body image. There appears to be little physical dependence, tolerance, or physical withdrawal syndrome associated with these drugs. Many executives who abuse these substances are under the age of forty and were initially introduced to these agents in the 1960s and 1970s during their high school and college years.

Opioids constitute the fourth category of abused drugs. This class includes opium, heroin, codeine, methadone, Demerol, and Dilaudid. Relatively few senior executives abuse these drugs;

those who do usually were being treated for a chronic pain disorder and became addicted to their prescription pain medication. These drugs produce physical dependence in all individuals who abuse them. The term *opium* comes from the Greek *opion*, which means juice. Opium is derived from a milky exudate of the unripe seed capsules of the poppy plant *Papaver somniferum*. The exudate is extracted, dried, and made into a powder that consists of opium and other naturally occurring alkaloids, including morphine, codeine, papaverine, and noscapine. A semisynthetic derivative of morphine is methadone, a substance used in a number of drug-rehabilitation programs.

The fifth and last category of abused drugs is the hallucinogens and includes phencyclidine (PCP), lysergic acid diethylamide (LSD), mescaline, and psilocybin. PCP was first introduced in the 1950s by Parke-Davis Company as a surgical anesthetic. Because it caused disorientation and general agitation, however, PCP was restricted to use as an animal anesthetic. It has the properties of both a psychedelic and a tranquilizer and can produce a strong psychological dependence without physical addiction. It is taken orally, sniffed, injected, or smoked. Referred to on the street as angel dust, crystal, peace, or peace weed, it causes changes in mood, hallucinations, delusions, confusion, and disorientation. The high lasts for four to six hours and is followed by a mild depression, irritability, and paranoia.

Mescaline is derived from the peyote cactus, psilocybin from mushrooms; LSD is man-made. These three drugs produce major changes in perceptions, thinking, and mood with visual distortions and hallucinations. A bad experience or "trip" can produce a sense of panic and psychosis. These drugs are also associated with flashbacks, or the experience of a drug in the drug-free state. They produce psychological rather than physical dependence. It is relatively rare to find a senior executive who is a serious abuser of these substances.

Origins of Victor's Drug Abuse

What were the factors that appeared to contribute to Victor's drug abuse? It is hard to say. Victor was a self-centered individual with a low frustration tolerance, a low threshold for un-comfortable inner tensions, and a disinterest in the needs and desires of others. His behavior showed him to be a rebellious, immature individual who sought attention in self-dramatizing behavior while being socially gregarious. Victor attempted to both deny and cover over his disturbing interpersonal and intrapsychic tensions, while both seeking praise and attention from authority figures and yet resenting and rebelling against his dependency on them. His preoccupation with superficialities and the praise and admiration of others left him bereft of a clear sense of his own identity and self-worth, further contributing to his drug abuse. Most likely as a child Victor, in spite of his material comforts, was depressed and lonely.

In sum, Victor was predisposed to the development of drug abuse because of (1) his constitutional endowment, which made his brain vulnerable biologically and psychologically to the repeated use of cocaine; (2) his deficit psychological functioning, including poor ego functioning, inadequate superego controls, problems with self-image and self-esteem, and poor impulse control; and (3) the encouragement of his subculture to experiment with drugs during his adolescence and young adulthood. The precipitates of Victor's drug use appeared to be (1) the long-term biological and psychological effects of continued cocaine use, (2) the continuing impact of deficient psychological structures and associated unresolved psychological conflicts, (3) the presence of occupational stress, (4) the high status and prestige of the drug, (5) the ready availability of the drug, and (6) Victor's capacity to afford the drug.

Recognizing the Executive Drug Abuser

The early warning signs of cocaine or other drug abuse in senior executives are similar to those for all other drug abusers. Depending on the type of drug and the route of ingestion, the drug abuser or drug-dependent individual will exhibit a variety of physical signs and symptoms. This may include agitation, changes in respiration, alterations in heart beat and pulse rate, nausea and vomiting, constipation, impotence, loss of menses, and problems with speech, gait, and general coordination. Look for senior executives who seem constantly agitated and unable to sit still. Take note of the senior executive who slurs her or his speech and seems periodically "out of it." In the intoxicated state the drug abuser or drug-dependent individual may also experience impairment of social or occupational functioning that results in deteriorating work performance, financial difficulties, and marital strife. Pay attention to the senior executive whose work performance deteriorates unexpectedly—for example, missed deadlines, sloppy work, and poorly written reports. Notice the senior executive who complains about chronic financial difficulties in spite of more than adequate compensation or the senior executive who appears to be living way above his or her means (due to excess income from selling drugs). Depending on the nature of the substance, the length of time of abuse, the amount consumed, the mental and physical state of the drug addict, and the abruptness of cessation of drug use, the drug-dependent individual will experience a withdrawal syndrome that can be mild to severe. Drug-dependent individuals in withdrawal will experience a variety of symptoms including nausea, vomiting, weakness, agitation, sweating, anxiety, depression, high blood pressure, sweating, diarrhea, changes in pupil size, fever, insomnia, delusions, hallucinations, and tremor of hands, tongue, and eyelids. Senior executives who suddenly begin to exhibit perspiration on their foreheads, develop a pronounced hand tremor, or have significant changes in their pupil size (or who suddenly wear sunglasses more frequently, complaining of "sensitive eyes") should be observed more closely. The medical complications of drug abuse and drug addiction include tetanus, viral hepatitis, AIDS, overdose, heart disease, tuberculosis, kidney disease, respiratory arrest, and sudden death. Long-term drug addiction can also cause irreversible brain damage, resulting in overall decrease in intellectual functioning, loss of memory, chronic delusions and hallucinations, changes in mood state, and overall changes in personality.

What were the telltale signs of Victor's drug-abuse problem? To begin with, he complained of a variety of physical symptoms, including fatigue, headaches, nausea, and insomnia.

He became depressed, irritable, withdrawn, and increasingly paranoid. He engaged in a variety of pathological behaviors related to his drug use, including absence from work for long periods of time during the day, unauthorized trips to Miami, and involvement in the sale of illegal drugs. Victor also developed problems with his concentration and his attention span, and he experienced weight loss without going on a diet. All of the above resulted in significant impairment of Victor's social and occupational functioning.

Commonly Asked Questions About Cocaine and Other Drug Abuse

Question Number One   Is it not a waste of time, energy, and resources to set up corporate programs to try and detect that rare senior executive drug abuser? No. Depending on the firm and the industry, drug abuse among senior executives may be uncommon but certainly not rare. Even one drug-addicted senior executive in a position of power and influence can wreak havoc if she or he is not detected early and treated for the problem.

Question Number Two   Can senior executives who have a cocaine or other drug problem really return to their former levels and responsibility within the firm after treatment? The issues of treatment of senior executives with alcoholism, drug abuse, or mental illness will be discussed in a later chapter, but the short answer is definitely yes.

Question Number Three   Is it not less serious for senior executives to be alcoholics than drug addicts? No. Alcohol is a drug in the barbiturate class with a significant risk of abuse, physical dependency, and deterioration in social and occupational functioning. Simply because alcohol use is legal in this country in no way modifies its abuse potential in senior executives or other individuals.

Question Number Four   Are drug abuse and addiction not so debilitating that senior executives who have this problem show obvious and unmistakable signs to their colleagues and friends? No. Examples abound of many highly capable and intelligent individuals who become dependent on drugs and who can function, if not in a superlative fashion, at least adequately for years without raising suspicions in their office colleagues. For some drug abusers the problem will only be obvious in the late stages of the disease.

Question Number Five Why is it that some senior executives and other individuals can use drugs such as cocaine and marijuana occasionally for "recreational" purposes without becoming addicted? No one knows for sure why some individuals are able to use drugs or alcohol occasionally without difficulty while others move on to drug abuse and addiction. Current research indicates that some individuals may have a biological or environmental predisposition to drug abuse and addiction. Given that it is not possible in advance to accurately predict who will and who will not eventually abuse drugs, the intelligent course of action is to avoid drug use altogether.

Question Number Six Where do senior executives and other drug abusers get their supply of drugs? Many senior executives and other drug abusers and addicts get their drugs from friends and colleagues, who may also be drug abusers or addicts. As a consequence, in any firm that has a significant drug problem among its employee or senior executive ranks, the probability that drugs are being bought and sold on site is very high.

Summary

Victor's cocaine use drove him to alienate his family and friends and to destroy a very promising career. Unfortunately, Victor is not alone. He is just one of many senior executives today who are suffering from the ravages of drug abuse and drug dependency. More will be said about the causes, treatment, and prevention of drug abuse and drug dependency in later chapters.

5

‗‗‗

Down and Almost Out:
The Story of
a Depressed Executive

Charlie slowly removed his bandages and extended his arms toward me to reveal two large, newly stitched knife wounds across each wrist. The dried blood was still caked on his forearms. Several hours prior to our meeting Charlie had been brought to the emergency room by ambulance after he was discovered by his wife, Alice, lying in the bathtub of their large suburban home, bleeding profusely. Had Charlie been more knowledgeable about the location of the major arteries of the wrist and forearm, he would not have lived to tell his story.

Charlie appeared to have everything going for him. He had recently been promoted to senior vice-president for human resources management for a large, well-known firm. He appeared to be happily married. He was the proud father of two thriving young girls. He was respected both in his company and in the community at large. And yet he attempted to take his own life. Why?

Charlie was suffering from a psychiatric illness called a major depressive episode. He was lucky. He survived his suicide attempt. There are many others who are not as fortunate. Nearly 30,000 individuals are successful at suicide every year in the United States. In fact, 50 percent of all suicides are committed by people, like Charlie, who are depressed, and over 70 percent of all individuals who are moderately to severely depressed have suicidal thoughts (Kaplan and Sadock, 1985, p. 794). How com-

50

mon is a serious depressive episode among senior executives? No one knows for sure. Depression is not unique to senior executives, nor is its manifestation in senior executives markedly different from that in, say, lawyers, architects, or physicians. Many accomplished, success-oriented individuals have an aversion to admitting that they are depressed, even when it appears obvious to the most casual observer. These high-powered individuals would rather be angry, frustrated, "overstressed," "burnt out," or just fatigued. To admit that one is depressed appears to be a sign of weakness; thus, the idea that one could be depressed simply does not come to mind. Unfortunately, the price of denial and inaction can be high:

> A fifty-five-year-old highly successful senior executive of a manufacturing firm became despondent after the funeral of his mother. He lost his motivation, drive, and powers of concentration. Six months later he prematurely terminated his successful career by retiring early.

> A fifty-two-year-old senior executive who had a family history of serious depression gradually became despondent and irritable. He began to have five or six drinks after work every evening at the local bar. One evening he was killed in a multicar accident on his way home.

> A sixty-five-year-old retired senior executive became despondent over large losses in the stock market and shot himself while at his desk.

> A forty-five-year-old upper-level executive, upset and depressed about not getting a promotion in the company, quit his job, began to drink heavily, and became involved in several extramarital affairs. After his wife filed for divorce, he admitted himself to an alcohol-rehabilitation center.

> A fifty-two-year-old upper-level executive was depressed over his poor future promotion prospects in his firm. He began investing in high-risk stocks and eventually lost half his net worth.

Nature of Depression

Major depressive episodes belong to a broader class of psychiatric illnesses called the affective disorders. This class of disorders includes the bipolar disorders, the major depressive episodes, cyclothymic disorders, dysthymic disorders, atypical bipolar disorders, and atypical depression. The affective disorders are disturbances that cause primarily an increase or decrease in one's activity accompanied by mood changes of either elation or depression. The affective disorders are the most frequent of all psychiatric illnesses. They cut across all socioeconomic groups and occupational categories. During their lifetime, as many as one in twenty Americans will become seriously depressed.

What are the causes of depression? No one single cause has been found to be responsible; instead, many factors appear to contribute to the development of depression. Research studies of families point to a genetic basis for some of the depressive disorders. Brain research has found that depressions can be associated with a deficiency of certain crucial neurochemicals, including norepinephrine and serotonin. Hormonal imbalances and abnormalities in the pituitary-adrenal axis also seem to contribute to the onset of depression. Individuals who experienced parental loss or poor mother-child interaction during childhood and who have problems with low self-esteem and poor self-image may be at higher risk for depression. Individuals who have problems with drug or alcohol abuse are also prone to substance-abuse-induced depression—a common cause of depression in senior executives. Alcohol or drug abuse can also be a result of depression—hence "drowning one's sorrows in drink."

Common Misconceptions About Executive Depression

Some senior executives have a number of misconceptions about depression and suicide that have prevented them from developing a fuller and more accurate understanding of the depressive disorders in the executive ranks.

Misconception Number One *Most senior executives appear to be well adjusted and not prone to depression.* Depression is something that can strike anyone. No one is immune. Those senior executives with a history of alcohol or drug abuse are especially at risk for the development of depression. Just because a senior executive does not wear a sad face or break out in tears does not mean that she or he is not depressed. Depression can present itself in a variety of forms, including manic behavior, alcoholism, drug abuse, impulsive behavior, irritability, and inappropriate and irrational decisions.

Misconception Number Two Depression occurs only after a highly stressful life event such as divorce, death in the family, or loss of job or position. Depression is not always precipitated by a stressful life event. In some individuals it occurs without any warning signs. Some individuals experience a chronic depression that can exist for years.

Misconception Number Three Getting out of a depressed state is simply a matter of willpower. This is not true. There are a number of different types of depression, some of which can be difficult to treat, particularly those that appear to have a genetic component.

Misconception Number Four Only the most irrational of individuals would contemplate or attempt suicide. Not true. Suicide is contemplated or attempted by individuals who may be irrational but also by individuals who are quite coherent.

Charlie's Story

As the firm's first black senior manager, Charlie felt torn between his empathy with the minority employees and their complaints and his allegiance to the management team. Although the firm was the largest employer in a three-county area that had a minority population of 20 percent, the firm's minority representation at the time that Charlie was hired stood at 2 percent. The employee work force was not unionized, and the company had a reputation for rewarding longevity and employee loyalty with job security rather than with competitive salaries and benefits. Starting hourly wages were significantly below the average for other employers in the community. The supervisors and managers were older white, male craftsmen who had worked their way up in the organization and who were inexperienced at supervising and managing diverse employee groups.

Although, because of Charlie's urging for the past two years, the firm had had an active affirmative action and equal opportunity program, progress was very slow, meeting with significant grumblings from the rest of the firm. The minority employees who had been with the firm less than two years still had higher rates of absenteeism, tardiness, and turnover than the employee population as a whole. Supervisors complained that the minority employees were "more trouble" than the other employees; the minority employees complained that the supervisors were prejudiced and insensitive. Recently, demand for the corporation's products had grown soft, and management announced that there would be significant reductions in the work force, particularly for employees with two or less years' tenure—virtually all of the minority employees.

A week after the announcement Charlie developed some tightness in his chest and began to worry that he might be developing a heart condition. He first went to the company physician, who examined him but could not detect any abnormality. The physician suggested that Charlie might be a little overstressed and should try to take it easy—perhaps even take a few days off. Charlie took the doctor's advice and stayed home for two days, but he felt even worse, and the chest tightness continued. He decided to go to a nationally respected heart specialist in Chicago. He took off three days from work and flew to Chicago, where he had a complete cardiac examination. No abnormality was found.

Back at work, Charlie felt increasingly frustrated and paralyzed. He no longer felt in control of his weekly departmental staff meeting; he felt disinterested and distracted. He began eating lunch at his desk rather than with his staff in the company cafeteria, which had been his usual pattern. He also dropped out of the weekend basketball games with his staff and stayed home from the annual company picnic. Charlie's appetite declined, and he began to have difficulty sleeping. In the mornings he felt tired and had difficulty getting out of bed. His concentration and attention span deteriorated. At home he appeared to be more irritable and on edge. He lost all interest in sex, began to drink more than usual, and complained of headaches and low back pain at work. The day before Charlie attempted suicide, he received a call from his boss, Hank Battery, who informed Charlie that due to budget constraints his department was being cut and he was being "temporarily" demoted.

The nature and sources of Charlie's depression were complex. He had a long history of bouts of depression. His father was known as a moody individual and hard drinker who would spend his paycheck on booze at the local bar. On a number of occasions Charlie's father was picked up by the police for disorderly conduct. In high school, Charlie was an A student and a member of the varsity wrestling team. In spite of his success, he often got into "blue moods." During these stressful times he would withdraw to his room and complain of vague stomach distress, which usually resulted in a day's absence from school. When he was fifteen, he broke his curfew and was "grounded" by his father for a month. Without much forethought Charlie went to the family medicine box, took out a large tin filled with aspirin, opened it, and swallowed its entire contents. Feeling sick to his stomach and guilty about what he had done, he told his mother about taking the aspirin. She rushed him to the local hospital, and his stomach was pumped. He stayed there overnight, was discharged the next day, and stayed in bed at home for the next couple of days recovering.

After an argument with his twelfth-grade history teacher, Charlie dropped out of high school against his parents' wishes and enlisted in the marines. After completing his military service, he moved back home. He worked at the local diner during the day and went to school at night to finish his high school education. Charlie went on to college at the local branch of the state university, majoring in business administration with a concentration in personnel management, and eventually graduated at the top of his class. Shortly after graduating he got married and began working for his current employer.

Origins of Depression

Research has uncovered a number of factors that appear to contribute to the development of depression. Studies have shown that relatives of patients with a major depressive disorder have a higher-than-expected rate of depression and other psychiatric disorders in comparison with the general population (Kaplan and Sadock, 1985, p. 779). Twin studies examining the different concordance rates in monozygotic twins (twins derived from one fertilized ovum) compared to dizygotic twins (twins derived from separate fertilized ova) avoided the difficulties of other studies in determining the differing influences of family environment and genetics. The investigators assumed that if there is a strong genetic component to unipolar illness, then monozygotic twins with the illness would show a significantly greater concordance rate than dizygotic twins. This was indeed the case. The monozygotic concordance rate of 54 percent was 2.8 times the dizygotic rate (Kaplan and Sadock, 1985, p. 762). In addition to the twin studies, other studies confirm that depressive disorders clearly have biological aspects. Patients who are seriously depressed have been discovered to have significant abnormalities in electrolyte balances; disturbed neurophysiology; dysfunctions in the autonomic nervous system; hormonal disturbances; abnormalities in the concentration, distribution, and function of neurotransmitters; and alterations in neuron cell receptor functioning. Further evidence of this biological thesis is the fact that antidepressants are quite effective in the treatment of major depressive disorders and appear to have very specific and localized impact on the brain's neurons and the neurotransmitters.

Other studies have also demonstrated that depressed individuals usually have a history of prior stressful life events that act as a trigger to the development of a depressive illness. It appears that depressed patients have weaknesses in their psychological structure that increase their vulnerability to major life crises. Depressed individuals seem to have significantly more problems with low self-esteem, poor self-image, harsh superego, and conflicting interpersonal relationships than the population as a whole. They also have significant problems with separation and loss, and as a legacy of their childhood they seem to have larger-than-average psychological reservoirs of anger, which frequently is turned against themselves in the form of self-destructive behavior and suicidal gestures. The research data as a whole seem to indicate a number of risk factors that contribute to the development of depression: (1) sex—twice as many women as men are depressed; (2) age—the onset of unipolar depression appears to occur most frequently in the midtwenties; (3) birth of a child—there are higher rates of serious psychiatric disorders, including depression, in women up to six months postpartum; (4) disruptive, chaotic, hostile, and generally negative family environment during childhood; (5) family depression; (6) personality characteristics of low stress tolerance, unassertiveness, dependency, and obsessional traits; (7) recent loss or exit of a significant person; and (8) absence of a fulfilling, satisfying intimate relationship.

What were the factors that contributed to Charlie's depression? Being the child of a depressed and alcoholic father, Charlie may have had a genetic endowment that made him vulnerable biologically and psychologically to the development of depression. As stated earlier, substance abuse and dependency and depression may share the same genetic and biological substrates. In addition, depressed and alcoholic parents frequently create emotionally depriving family environments for their offspring. It is likely that Charlie's father was seriously depressed during most of his life and chose to medicate himself with alcohol, which, unfortunately, made his depression worse and increased the emotional deprivation of the family. The psychological underpinnings of Charlie's depression became clearer as he began to open up during the course of his hospitalization. He admitted to having had feelings of depression and anger off and on since his childhood. He remembered that during his upbringing he always felt a little hungry, both nutritionally and emotionally. He felt lonely and isolated as a child and perceived his father as an overly harsh disciplinarian who was emotionally cold and distant. Charlie said that his father would always disappoint him by making promises that he did not keep. Charlie's athletic exploits and academic achievements were in part motivated by the desire to get his father's attention—unfortunately, to little avail. Charlie thought that his father cared more about the bottle than he did about his own son. Charlie admitted that, as a way to both vent his anger and get his father's attention, he would periodically defy his father's authority. An example was Charlie's overdose when he was grounded by his father for a month. The gesture was also an attention-seeking attempt to gain the upper hand and manipulate his parents into allowing him to do what he wanted.

Charlie admitted that his problems with authority spilled over into his work life. He said that he never felt very good about himself and that he overworked in part to counteract feelings of personal inadequacy. His desire to excel on the job was also related to a continuing displaced desire to win the praise and love of his father, while his animosity toward the whites in the corporation was a displacement of his feelings of rejection and hostility. Charlie felt that he had to prove something to the whites, just as he felt he had to prove something to his father. Charlie's view of himself was supported by the results of his psychological testing. They showed Charlie to be an intensely depressed, needy, and insecure individual with significant problems accepting authority, a low self-image, a harsh and punitive superego, and poor impulse control. He looked with dread and apprehension toward the future. He felt that he was psychologically unraveling and felt depleted and helpless in managing the stresses in his life. Charlie defended against conflictual feelings about his father and other authority figures by employing relatively primitive psychological defenses, including acting out, projection, denial, displacement, repression, and somatization.

What was the relationship between the stresses and conflicts that Charlie experienced at work and his depression? Did his demanding job cause his depression? Probably not. Charlie's genetic endowment, biological predisposition, and unresolved psychological conflicts were more fertile ground for his depression. These factors caused Charlie to behave inappropriately at work, which in turn made his job more stressful and difficult.

His desiring to please and be accepted while at the same time resenting conformity to the wishes and demands of authority figures got in the way of his effective performance on the job.

In sum, Charlie was predisposed to the development of a major depressive disorder because of (1) his genetic endowment, which made him vulnerable biologically and psychologically to certain life stressors; and (2) his early childhood experiences, which resulted in deficient psychological development, a harsh and punitive superego, problems with self-image and self-esteem, rigid and immature defense mechanisms, poor impulse control, and significant unresolved psychological conflicts. The precipitates of Charlie's depression appeared to be (1) the long-term biological and psychological effects of continued alcohol use and (2) the continuing impact of deficient psychological structures and associated unresolved psychological conflicts.

Early Warning Signs of Depression

Seriously depressed individuals like Charlie are quite different from individuals who experience transient sadness or temporary emotional distress. A major depressive episode lasts longer, has a wider range of symptoms, and significantly interferes with an executive's social and occupational functioning. By Charlie's account, his depression had probably been going on for at least six months and possibly longer, and it made him less effective at work and at home. Seriously depressed senior executives often experience the signs and symptoms of depression without having any conscious awareness that they are seriously depressed.

Exactly what were the signs and symptoms of Charlie's depression? First, he experienced insomnia, loss of appetite, and a decrease in his level of energy. He did not have much interest in food. He lost ten pounds without even trying. He had difficulty falling asleep and often woke up in the middle of the night. He complained of feeling fatigued all the time—just no get up and go. The lethargy appeared to be worst in the morning, when he had to get out of bed to go to work.

Second, Charlie complained of problems in his attention span and his concentration. He had difficulty paying attention in his staff meetings and seemed to be distracted all the time. Third, he lost interest in the daily activities of living, particularly those activities from which he used to derive pleasure. He no longer ate lunch with his staff in the company cafeteria, did not play basketball with the guys, skipped the company picnic, was no longer interested in involving himself in the life of the family, and was not interested in sex. Fourth, Charlie experienced a variety of physical ailments and complaints, including chest tightness, lower back pain, and headaches, that appeared to have no associated physical abnormality. Although the mechanism is unclear, physical ailments that appear during the course of a major depressive episode seem to be related to the illness; when the depression is treated, these ailments frequently diminish in severity and intensity, if not disappearing entirely. Fifth, Charlie became socially isolated; he was simply not interested in associating with people. He preferred to stay by himself, closed in, away from others, including his staff, his family, and his boss.

Sixth, Charlie had active suicidal thoughts and exhibited poor impulse control by making an actual suicide attempt. Seventh, he felt a sense of frustration, anger, helplessness, and hopelessness, particularly about his work situation. Over time Charlie felt powerlessness and paralysis. Eighth, Charlie experienced a disappointment and loss—the loss of his position and status within the firm. Last of all, Charlie increased his consumption of alcoholic beverages. He went from one beer a night to three or four.

Charlie had many of the classical signs and symptoms of a major depressive disorder. Seriously depressed individuals also experience decreased or increased appetite, which can lead to significant weight loss or gain. In addition, depressed individuals commonly experience significant disturbances in their sleep pattern and are plagued by either insomnia or its opposite, hypersomnia, or sleeping too much. Feeling sluggish, slowed down, and uninterested in daily activities are common complaints of seriously depressed individuals. Some also report an increase in anxiety exhibited by hand wringing, pacing, and general restlessness. Some seriously depressed individuals suddenly lose their sense of competence and confidence in their talents and abilities. They behave as if they are no longer familiar with or knowledgeable about their jobs. They often complain that they are having difficulty thinking clearly or quickly about abstract or conceptual issues. They have difficulty paying attention, they lose their concentration, and they become forgetful. In some instances they are indecisive, exhibit poor business judgment, and act impulsively, which often results in inappropriate, ill-informed, or ill-advised decisions.

Colleagues of depressed senior executives often notice that something is wrong but remain quiet out of respect for the individual's privacy. Spouses notice that the individual is less talkative than usual and appears to be more pessimistic about the future than circumstances would warrant. This sense of haplessness and pessimism can, as Charlie's case amply illustrates, turn into a more active desire to take one's own life. Because depression is considered a sign of weakness, many senior executives will either deny that there is anything wrong or delay getting adequate professional help, hoping that the passage of time will cure all. Stress is a much more palatable concept than depression. Senior executives often deal with stress by working harder or taking an ill-timed vacation or business trip to an attractive spot. They will also increase their indulgence in alcoholic beverages, prescription drugs like Valium or Librium, or illegal substances like cocaine. Some senior executives attempt to drown their sorrows in extramarital affairs, risky business ventures, or impulsive career changes.

Summary

Charlie exhibited the classical signs and symptoms of a major depressive disorder. The diagnosis may not always be so clear. Many individuals have only a few of the signs and symptoms that Charlie exhibited. Others do not give good or adequate histories, forget things that happened, and deny crucial events. They are sometimes uncooperative and resistant to telling their life stories to a psychiatrist—a perfect stranger—because they are afraid they will be certified "crazy." They often present a confusing picture of symptoms that points to the possibility of several interacting psychiatric disorders. For instance, depression can lead one to drink, while, conversely, the consumption of large amounts of alcohol can result in depression. Depression can also be associated with schizophrenia, be the result of a brain tumor or a metabolic disorder, or be caused by the taking of prescribed medication for an unrelated medical disorder. Charlie was seriously depressed and nearly ended his life because of depression—a tragic but, unfortunately, not uncommon outcome for individuals who suffer from undiagnosed and untreated depression. More will be said in later chapters about the management and treatment of senior executives who become seriously depressed.

6

━━━━━━━━━━━━━━━━━━━━━━━━━━━━━━━━━━━━━━━

Soaring:
The Story of
a Manic Executive

Jerry was a thirty-one-year-old attorney and a highly re-garded senior vice-president for government relations for a high-technology firm. He was also a manic-depressive who decided to stop taking his lithium carbonate. He ended up in the hospital after being picked up by the police in the company of a woman who was not his wife at one o'clock in the morning. They were both intoxicated and had been found wading without their clothes in the reflecting pool of the Washington Monument. On further questioning, the police determined that Jerry was out of touch with reality. His wife, Sarah, also an attorney, was called immediately and admitted Jerry to the hospital at three o'clock in the morning.

Nature of Manic-Depressive Illness

Individuals, like Jerry, who are afflicted with manic-depressive illness (MDI), also known as bipolar disorder, exhibit severe disturbance of mood marked with unpredictable swings into either depression or elation. MDI belongs to a larger group of mental illnesses called the affective disorders. All affective disorders have in common a severe disturbance in mood, with significant impairment in occupational and social functioning. There are three types of bipolar disorders: bipolar, manic; bipolar, depressed; and bipolar, mixed. Bipolar, manic and bipolar, depressed individuals have primarily manic and depressed episodes, respectively. The bipolar, mixed individual has acute episodes with elements of both mania and depression. The bipolar individual usually experiences the first episode of either mania or depression during adolescence or the early twenties. Episodes of either mania or depression recur on an average of every 2.7 to nine years, with more frequent episodes in the later years (Kaplan and Sadock, 1985, p. 765). Although bipolar illness is characterized by mood swings between depression and elation, it is uncommon for bipolar individuals to have an equal number of manic and depressive episodes that alternate in precise sequence. Instead, bipolar individuals usually have a predominance of either manic attacks or depressive attacks. The incidence of bipolar disorder in the United States is estimated to be 300 cases per 100,000.

No one knows how many senior executives are afflicted with this disorder. For reasons that are not entirely clear, bipolar illness seems to be more common in individuals of high intellectual ability such as professionals, high-level business executives, scientists, and writers. A study of patients in a German psychiatric clinic discovered that bipolar illness was three times more common in the higher social classes than in the population at large. This is also consistent with the U.S. Army's experience in World War II, where bipolar illness was found to be three times more common in American officers than in enlisted men. The cause of manic-depressive illness is not known (Kolb, 1977, p. 441). Biological and psychological factors appear to play a significant role. Data from studies of twins, affected families, and population surveys suggest a genetic predisposition. Other studies have pointed to a disturbance of or imbalance in the brain's neurochemistry.

Jerry's Story

Jerry began to have problems soon after he was put in charge of the lobbying effort to try to convince Congress to impose trade restrictions on his firm's Japanese competitors. A trade-restriction

bill that was sponsored by the leaders of both parties had recently been introduced in the Senate—not a small feat consider-
ing that the White House had already gone on record opposing
all protectionist legislation.

No one in the firm knew that Jerry had a long history of
manic-depressive illness or that he had been taking lithium carbonate four times a day for a number of years. Jerry soon became a whirlwind of activity with his new responsibility. During
the course of an average day he would set up meetings, arrange
evening receptions, coordinate grass-roots letter campaigns, lobby
key congressional leaders, map out day-to-day strategy, orches-
trate lobbying efforts with the senior management, and research
topics for briefings to key White House staffers. Shortly after
Jerry started his around-the-clock lobbying effort, he decided to
"temporarily" stop taking his lithium because he felt that it
slowed him down.

About a month after Jerry went off his lithium, his colleagues began to notice that his words increasingly came out in
a torrent and his ideas became increasingly jumbled and discon-
nected. Jerry always seemed to be in an extraordinarily good
mood—laughing and joking with the staff and playing practical
jokes on the secretaries. He maintained a very high level of optimism in spite of the fact that most observers on the Hill had
concluded that his bill had very little chance of passing. Although
Jerry maintained his jovial demeanor, he became increasingly in-
tolerant of any criticism. At one moment he would be joking, and
the next minute he would fly into a rage, yelling at a member of
the staff for no apparent reason. After one such occasion Jerry
felt so guilty about what he had done to his staffer that he went
out that afternoon and bought the staffer a $5,000 mink coat,
charging it to the corporate expense account. The staff member
returned the coat the next day without Jerry's knowledge.

On another occasion Jerry offered to buy a staff member
a brand-new $18,000 sports car on his personal line of credit be-
cause the staff member had been arriving at work late due to car
difficulties. Jerry bought season tickets to Bullets' games for the
entire staff, even though there were only two staff members
who were basketball fans. Jerry also came up with the idea of

flying the entire membership of the Senate subcommittee to the Bahamas for the weekend before the vote to help them relax.

During his daily staff meetings Jerry would often pace the floor and carry on a conversation with himself while listening to others give a presentation. On many nights Jerry would stay at the office until 3:00 A.M. working on his plans for the next day. He began to drink more than usual, and he often became loud and boisterous at receptions. At one event he greatly offended the wife of a senior senator by commenting on the size of her derriere. Jerry became more distracted and irritable at home and reckless with his driving. Several days before he was discovered in the reflecting pool of the Washington Monument, he began to invest the family savings in highly speculative Florida real-estate deals, much to the consternation of his wife.

Jerry was a descendant of a well-known New England family. Several buildings at a prestigious New England university carried the family name, and several of his relatives had held high positions in government at the state and national levels. Jerry was the youngest of three boys. His brothers were graduates of well-known New England boarding schools. Jerry's oldest brother was a tenured university professor, and his middle brother was an ophthalmologist in private practice in the western suburbs of Boston. Jerry's father came from a background of wealth and privilege and was educated at the best private schools in New England. He was now a partner in a large, well-established law firm in Boston. Jerry's mother, Billi, was a very attractive woman who also came from a prominent family and was educated at an exclusive all-girl private academy. She was a devoted wife and mother who raised her children while staying very active in civic affairs. She sat on the boards of several well-known cultural institutions in Boston, and on several occasions she was active in the political campaigns of close relatives.

In spite of their accomplishments, many of Jerry's relatives were mentally ill. Billi's mother had a long history of mental illness, requiring her to spend extended periods at one of New England's well-known private psychiatric hospitals. Jerry would visit his grandmother with his mother on Sundays during her hospitalizations, and she would talk incessantly and always appeared to be in great spirits in spite of her confinement. Jerry's great-uncle killed himself in his early twenties, and several first cousins were diagnosed as manic-depressives and were currently on lithium.

As a child Jerry was known for moving at twice the speed of his peers. His teachers considered him a gifted student, a talented musician, and an outstanding athlete. He was a very gregarious person who enjoyed enormous popularity among his classmates. In his senior year he was president of the student senate, president of the senior class, captain of the varsity squash team, and editor of the school newspaper, all while maintaining an A– average. When Jerry was excited about a project, he would accelerate his speech, which earned him the nickname "motor-mouth."

In college Jerry continued to do well. He excelled at squash, was a very good student, and had an active social life. In his junior year his grandmother died suddenly of a massive stroke during one of her psychiatric hospitalizations. After the funeral Jerry became increasingly agitated. He began to miss classes and stayed up late night after night working at the campus computer center. He thought he had figured out a way to beat Wall Street. He began to make long-distance calls to various private investors around the country, trying to convince them to purchase his new program. One Friday in the middle of the spring term Jerry went home for a weekend visit and did not return; instead, he spent eight weeks in a local private psychiatric hospital, where he was diagnosed as manic-depressive. He was stabilized on lithium and returned to school the following fall.

Jerry had two other manic episodes. He had one episode during the summer after his second year in law school. After his exams Jerry became manic and had to spend a month in the hospital. He also became manic during the first year after taking the job with his current employer and was hospitalized for three weeks. No one knew he was a manic-depressive except his family. He always told people that he was in the hospital for a back problem. Before each manic episode Jerry had stopped taking his lithium without the knowledge of his family or his prescribing physician.

As a staff attorney with his current firm, Jerry showed his talents early by obtaining a very favorable out-of-court settlement of a major product-liability suit. He so impressed the senior management that within three years he became head of the corporate legal department and was thought to be a natural choice to head up the new Washington office. Jerry became the youngest senior vice-president in his firm's history, accepting his new position just after celebrating his twenty-ninth birthday.

Causes of Manic-Depressive Illness

Research data suggest several factors responsible for the development of bipolar illness. From a genetic point of view, bipolar illness is nearly twenty-five times as common among the siblings of bipolar patients as in the population as a whole. Adoption studies have discovered that the biological parents of adopted children are nearly three times as likely to develop affective disorder as the adoptive parents. Biochemical studies now point to changes in the processes of electrolyte metabolism, electrophysiology, and neuroendocrinology as being contributors to the development of bipolar illness. Psychologically speaking, bipolar individuals appear to have certain personality traits in common, including self-confidence, aggressiveness, self-assertiveness, and ease with people.

Jerry's decision to stop taking his lithium clearly played a major role in his most recent acute manic illness. The relapse rate for bipolar individuals who stop taking their lithium is quite high. In addition, the day-to-day stresses of the job were contributing factors in the development of this latest manic episode. Both Jerry's wife and his boss denied what was happening to Jerry until it was too late. Jerry's wife knew that he required lithium and that he had a history of discontinuing the medication, particularly under stress, but she did not strongly encourage him to continue taking it. During his hospitalization Jerry opened up more. He described himself as generally being a happy-go-lucky individual who had high standards for himself but who sometimes felt that he was not working hard enough to achieve his goals. He admitted frequently resenting taking his lithium because it made him feel like he was in a straitjacket. He felt he was more creative and better able to go full speed in pursuit of his goals when off the medication. In sum, Jerry was predisposed to the development of bipolar illness because of a strong family history and genetic endowment that made him vulnerable. The precipitates of his illness appeared to be (1) the cessation of his lithium and (2) the stresses of his job.

Signs and Symptoms of Manic-Depressive Illness

Early in manic-depressive illness, senior executives in the manic phase may be indistinguishable from other senior executives who are outgoing, gregarious, and extroverted. Combined with their generally high level of intelligence, many manic-depressive senior executives, like Jerry, are surprisingly creative and productive. Approximately 33 percent of bipolar individuals experience three or more episodes of either mania or depression over the course of a lifetime. A bipolar individual may have a very unexpected episode of the illness, even while on medication, after many years of stability and successful treatment.

What are the early warning signs of a manic episode in a manic-depressive executive? First, there is a change in the senior executive's mood, with a surprising upbeat attitude and optimism alternating with sudden outbursts of anger, all of which seem inappropriate and out of place. For example, Jim, a senior marketing executive in the beginning phases of a manic episode, talked incessantly about new business ventures and began calling up his colleagues at three in the morning to discuss his new ideas. When his ideas were challenged, Jim would fly into a rage, heaping abuse on whoever was present. The manic senior executive will exhibit great bursts of energy, showing little need for sleep while becoming involved with an extraordinary range of activities, resulting in overextension and poor judgment. For example, Alex, a senior executive with a history of MDI, decided to take up the piano and the violin at the age of forty-two, began running at four in the morning, started an investment newsletter in his spare time, and purchased gifts for all the office staff.

The bipolar senior executive in the manic phase will also show changes in speech and flow of thoughts with increased distractibility. Bill, a manic senior executive, began speaking rapidly and loudly. His speech was often filled with irreverent comments, jokes, and barbs, and it was often very difficult to interrupt him. His thoughts rapidly skipped from one idea to another, making it very difficult to follow his train of thought. He was easily distracted, as his attention shifted quickly from one project to another. Some manic senior executives, in the later stages of their illness, will begin to experience auditory hallucinations and delusional thoughts. John, a manic senior executive, began to hear "otherworldly" voices speaking to him, and he began to believe that he had special powers and was being persecuted by unknown forces. Without treatment, which usually involves hospitalization and medication, the manic senior executive will become increasingly more disorganized and bizarre, posing a risk of possible harm to himself and others.

What were the early warning signs of Jerry's manic episode? The first indications of his manic state were his jovial mood, practical jokes, excessive cheerfulness, boundless energy, overblown optimism, and heightened self-confidence. Second, Jerry exhibited unpredictable mood swings from cheerfulness to anger. Third, he made inappropriate comments to the staff and to strangers at receptions. Fourth, he acted inappropriately in terms of his long-distance telephone calls, spending of money, and giving of gifts. Fifth, he increased his drinking both at home and at work. Sixth, he began to show poor judgment about matters at the office and about personal investments. Finally, he became delusional, as evidenced by his holding bizarre beliefs in the face of reality.

In contrast to Jerry's manic phase, bipolar individuals in the depressed phase have all the signs and symptoms associated with a major depressive disorder. These include poor appetite, sleeplessness, low self-esteem, poor judgment, lack of insight, poor concentration, shortened attention span, poor memory, physical complaints, fatigue, and suicidal thoughts. Because the signs and symptoms of the bipolar depressed phase are identical to those of a major depressive disorder, it is sometimes hard to differentiate between the two. Depressed individuals who are truly bipolar must have had at least one manic episode in their lifetime to be formally diagnosed as having manic-depressive disorder.

Commonly Asked Questions About Executives with Manic-Depressive Illness

Question Number One Do senior executives with manic-depressive illness differ in any way from others afflicted with this disorder? No. For the most part, senior executives with this illness exhibit the full range of symptoms, respond to the same treatment, and generally have the same prognosis as others in the society. Senior executives with MDI who are able to continue with a successful career in management generally do not fall into the small subgroup of manic-depressives who have the most severe form of the illness, which may be refractory to standard treatments. Persons with the most severe form of MDI may have difficulty living outside of a psychiatric facility.

Question Number Two Do manic-depressive senior executives have an easier or a more difficult time successfully pursuing a career in management than do senior executives recovering from alcoholism, drug abuse, or depression? Even though there is no cure for manic-depressive illness, successfully treated bipolar senior executives may be indistinguishable from their professional colleagues and peers. In fact, some of the world's most creative and successful individuals have been manic-depressives. In the large majority of successfully treated and maintained manic-depressive individuals, there is no long-term deterioration in performance or quality of life in comparison to senior executives and others with significant long-term problems with alcoholism, drug abuse, or depression.

Question Number Three Once a senior executive with MDI has a manic episode, how long will it last, will the individual need to be hospitalized, and when will the individual be able to return to work? Manic episodes can last from several days to several months, depending on the individual. An attack of mania usually begins with a mild symptomatology and escalates, if untreated, to a full-blown major manic episode. Once a manic episode has begun, affected individuals will probably need to be hospitalized from several days to several weeks. After the manic episode has been adequately treated and the manic-depressive executive has been released from the hospital, he or she may return to work.

Question Number Four   Will the manic-depressive senior executive continue to have manic episodes, and how often will they occur? Many manic-depressive individuals will continue to have either manic or depressive episodes even while taking adequate doses of medication. Some manic-depressive individuals will have only one manic or depressive episode once every ten years or more, while others will have an episode every few months. The most common cause of a recurrence of a manic or depressive episode is noncompliance with prescribed medication.

Question Number Five   Does the stress in the corporate environment contribute to the development of a manic episode in a bipolar senior executive? There is no solid evidence that stress itself is responsible for the onset of a manic or depressive episode or that bipolar senior executives in high-pressure corporate environments are any more liable to manic or depressive episodes than, say, artists or writers who have MDI.

Question Number Six   Are bipolar senior executives potentially violent or dangerous? The vast majority of bipolar individuals are not potentially violent or dangerous. Only that small fraction of bipolar individuals who, in the throes of a major manic attack, develop auditory hallucinations and paranoid delusional thinking may pose a risk of harm to themselves and others.

Summary

Jerry was a manic-depressive in the manic phase. His disease was undetected until he became so impaired that his behavior jeopardized the goals and aims of his organization. Although there is currently no cure for manic-depressive illness, accurate and timely diagnosis with appropriate treatment and follow-up can significantly reduce the chances of a manic or depressive episode. More will be said later about the detection, treatment, and prevention of manic-depressive disorders.

7

~~~~~~

The Enemies Within:
The Story of
a Psychotic Executive

Ralph was a thirty-two-year-old software engineer and vice-president of software development for a large high-technology firm. He had just been released after an eight-week stay at a private psychiatric hospital. The reason for Ralph's hospitalization? "I tried to kill my boss."

Seven months prior to his hospitalization Ralph began to appear increasingly tired and disheveled at work. He began to spend more and more of his time in his office alone. He became periodically confused and forgetful about the sequence of daily tasks. Often he would lapse into vague and rambling monologues about the "specialness" of the project he was working on. He accused various members of the development team of not pulling their weight and made references to saboteurs in the organization who were attempting to undermine his work. At one point Ralph abruptly fired one of the programmers from a project because he was convinced, in spite of evidence to the contrary, that the programmer "was leaking" proprietary information about Ralph's project to competitors.

Ralph became increasingly more irritable and unpredictable in his behavior during the last week before his hospitalization. He stopped riding the building elevator and instead walked up and down the eleven flights of stairs to and from his office, insisting that he just needed "more exercise." He changed the time and location of the staff meeting every week, explaining that it was good to "keep people off balance." At staff meetings Ralph insisted that he sit closest to the door. He had the locks changed on his office door three times in one week, offering the rationale that "security needed to be tightened" at the firm. When his boss, Harvey, attempted to talk to Ralph about his behavior, Ralph denied that there was anything wrong. On the day of Ralph's admission to the hospital he barged into Harvey's office unannounced and demanded to know why Harvey had his phone tapped and why he had assigned the managers in the office next door to spy on him. Ralph insisted that he could hear the managers through his office wall talking about him and making plans to do him in. As Harvey tried to reason with him, Ralph pulled a .37-caliber revolver out of the pocket of his sports coat. He aimed directly at Harvey and demanded that Harvey stop spying on him. Harvey became quiet. He then agreed to stop spying on Ralph while inching slowly in Ralph's direction. He was able to get close enough to Ralph to grab the barrel of the revolver. A struggle ensued, and the gun went off. Fortunately, no one was injured. Harvey managed to wrestle the gun away from Ralph and physically subdued him until the company security police arrived. Later that afternoon Ralph was admitted to the local private psychiatric hospital.

Things had been very different two years ago, when Harvey had hired Ralph and given him a mandate to develop state-of-the-art software products that would create and dominate new markets. With the promise of excellent compensation, freedom from corporate meddling, and royalty participation in newly developed products, Ralph was able to recruit a group of young, aggressive, and very talented programmers and software-development engineers, who quickly became the envy of the industry. They liked to wear jeans and work shirts and were unorthodox in their work habits. Ralph and his team had been working intensively on the project for the past two years. The software product targeted the powerful user in the corporate setting and exploited all the features of the most advanced microcomputers on the market. The product functioned well in a local-area-network environment and allowed users to be more productive with number-oriented tasks. In spite of its power and sophistication, the product was very user friendly, with an excellent graphics interface. Initial projections by the marketing group indicated that it would be very well received and had the potential of capturing 50 percent of a market that was estimated to grow to $250 million within five years. In spite of the product's promise, rumors circulated weekly that other software firms were preparing to introduce competitive products into the market. Time was clearly of the essence.

During his hospitalization, Ralph recalled the hectic times at work months before his breakdown:

> I really had a lot of myself invested in this software project, but I just didn't seem to be getting the breaks. I started popping amphetamines to try and keep myself alert. During the last month before my hospitalization, several serious bugs appeared in the program, which threatened to significantly delay its delivery date for the third time and destroy my firm's projected quarterly earnings.
>
> During the next several weeks I began spending all my time working on that program. I had very little social life as it was, but it was totally shot during that time. I got some help from programmers from other parts of the division and the corporation who were temporarily assigned to my development team. I canceled leave time for all members of my team until the project was completed. When I got too tired to work any more, I would take brief catnaps on my office sofa. For meals I ordered pizza and cheese steak sandwiches to go from an all-night pizza parlor close to the office. Every couple of days my roommates would bring me a clean set of clothes, and I took my showers at the fitness club I belonged to two blocks from the office. I guess I finally just fell apart.

This was not the first time that psychiatric illness had entered the lives of Ralph and his family. When Ralph was four years old, his father committed suicide at the age of forty-two.

He had been known as a brilliant but eccentric engineer who was in and out of psychiatric hospitals shortly before his death. After his father's death, Ralph and his mother moved back to the small town in Ohio where she had grown up to live with Ralph's grandparents. Ralph enjoyed his childhood years. His grandparents were warm and caring people who looked after him during the day and after school until his mother came home. He spent many happy times with his mother in the evenings and on weekends, the only times she was free from her job as a teacher in the local public school system. His mother remarried, to another public school teacher, when Ralph was in fifth grade.

Ralph was smaller than his peers and was very shy. He had very few playmates, and in spite of his grandparents' encouragement to seek out neighborhood children, he seemed to prefer playing by himself. His favorite pastime was making believe he had a houseful of playmates, with whom he would talk and play. Every now and then Ralph would imagine his father had come back to life and was playing with him. During his elementary school years, Ralph was a gifted learner and good student to whom schoolwork generally came very easily. He often became bored in class and would daydream while staring out the window. Only with great encouragement from his teachers would he participate in class. When he did speak up, he spoke haltingly, staring down at his shoes or up at the ceiling. In spite of his shyness, Ralph's teachers considered him a good child and a gifted if somewhat overly compliant student.

Because of his high aptitude Ralph had skipped two grades by the time he reached high school. As a high school sophomore he began taking college-level math courses at the local university but did not date or involve himself in sports or extracurricular activities. Ralph's outstanding high school record helped him to win a full scholarship to one of the nation's leading technical institutes. It marked the first time that he had ever lived away from home.

Although Ralph's scores on the aptitude tests won him advanced standing to sophomore status, he had difficulty from the beginning adjusting to the new environment. During his first semester Ralph started to think that his professors were out to get him and that someone was putting mind-altering drugs in the cafeteria food. He believed that he could hear others in the next room talking about him. He also began to believe that some alien being was controlling his thoughts or trying to put strange thoughts into his head, that his thoughts were being broadcast over a loudspeaker, and that he had developed a special power to read people's minds. He was eventually hospitalized for six weeks at the suggestion of the school physician.

After that episode Ralph dropped out of school for a year, moved back home, and worked at a variety of odd jobs. His family physician kept him on Stelazine—a major tranquilizer—for about a year. After a year Ralph, on the advice of his physician, stopped taking the medication, in spite of the fact that periodically he thought he detected the presence of another "being" with "the powers of my sixth sense." He worked at odd jobs until the following academic year, when he enrolled as a full-time student at a branch of the state university. During that year a math professor introduced him to the world of microcomputers. He became so interested that he switched his major from math to computer science. Ralph was a loner on campus, preferring to spend his free time outside of classes in the computer room at the university, and during the summer he was able to master several computer languages. He graduated with a straight-A average in computer sciences.

After graduation, Ralph was hired as a computer programmer for a local firm, and he continued to live at home. Although it was a good job, he felt dissatisfied with the restrictions on his creative freedom. After two years with the firm he enrolled full time in an MBA program at the local university. Although he felt the MBA experience useful, he was dissatisfied with the lack of rigor in the program and the lack of emphasis on technical expertise. He often finished his assignments early and spent a good deal of time in the computer room playing games and thinking up ideas for new software.

Ralph graduated near the top of his class and was heavily recruited by a number of *Fortune* 500 firms. He decided to accept an offer to work as a programmer for a new firm in California. He shared a three-bedroom apartment with two of his colleagues, who also worked for computer firms. Ralph became quite successful at his new job, developing several new programs for the business microcomputer market that became overnight sensations. Unfortunately, his compensation did not keep pace with his growing success and reputation in the market. When Harvey called and asked Ralph to come on board as the new vice-president of software development at substantially increased compensation, he jumped at the chance and moved back east to accept the position.

Nature of Schizophrenia

What was Ralph's problem? Why did he make a serious threat on the life of his boss? Ralph was a paranoid schizophrenic. Schizophrenia is a major psychiatric disorder that is common to all societies and cultures around the world. Approximately 1 percent of the American population is schizophrenic. The illness strikes men and women equally, usually in their late teens and early twenties. Although the illness is more common in individuals with a lower socioeconomic status, it also strikes individuals in the upper socioeconomic classes, including doctors, lawyers, engineers, politicians, and executives.

More than two million individuals are diagnosed as schizophrenic in the United States, equal to nearly half the population of the city of New York. This number nearly equals the number of people who live in "Oregon, Mississippi, and Kansas, or in Wyoming, Vermont, Delaware, and Hawaii combined. On any given day there are 600,000 people with schizophrenia under active treatment (in the United States)" (Torrey, 1983, p. 1). Schizophrenia is actually a group of related psychiatric conditions. The types of schizophrenia include disorganized, catatonic, paranoid, undifferentiated, and residual. As a group these illnesses have a devastating impact on the mental status and psychological health of the afflicted individual. In spite of the advances made in diagnosis and treatment, "the incidence of schizophrenia in the United States has probably remained unchanged, at least for the past 100 years and possibly throughout the entire history of the country, despite tremendous socioeconomic and population changes" (Kaplan and Sadock, 1981, p. 299).

Schizophrenia can be relatively sudden in onset, bizarre in its manifestations, difficult to treat, and chronic in its course. It strikes down individuals at the onset of their most productive years. Contrary to common perception, schizophrenia does not refer to a multiple personality, which characterizes another psychiatric disorder. The schizophrenic individual is not split into separate personalities, such as Dr. Jekyll and Mr. Hyde or Sybil's multiple selves; it is the parts of the individual's mind that are split and fragmented. It is a real disease—as real as cancer, diabetes, or heart disease. Like many other diseases, it has multiple causes and a variety of treatments.

As Ralph's case demonstrates, schizophrenia grossly distorts thinking processes, severely alters mood states, and significantly impairs social and occupational functioning. The diagnostic criteria from *DSM-III-R* (American Psychiatric Association, 1987) more precisely defines schizophrenia as a mental disorder in which the patient may experience delusional thinking, auditory hallucinations, illogical thinking, absence of emotional response, inability to function adequately in either a social or an occupational role, difficulties in verbal communication, and peculiar or bizarre behavior. The illness must have begun before the age of forty-five, and the patient must have had some symptoms of the disorder for at least six months. Fortunately, schizophrenia is very uncommon among executives, managers, and administrators. More so than depression, manic-depressive illness, or even alcoholism or drug abuse, schizophrenia devastates those mental abilities that the executive needs most—clear thinking, the ability to accurately assess reality, think clearly and abstractly, have insight and intuition, and make sound judgments and quick decisions. Because schizophrenia strikes relatively early, it debilitates early and abruptly ends many careers before they have really begun.

Early Warning Signs of Schizophrenia

What were the symptoms of Ralph's mental illness? During the six months prior to his hospitalization, Ralph's speech rambled and became vague. He lost interest in his appearance. He became confused and gradually lost his ability to think clearly, rationally, abstractly, and conceptually. He lost his business judgment and began to make inappropriate management decisions, such as firing one of his programmers for insufficient reasons. He became increasingly paranoid, suspicious, and inappropriately angry at both his staff and his boss. He made unfounded accusations. He began to develop a whole set of strange, unusual, and bizarre beliefs or delusions in spite of evidence to the contrary. He believed that there were saboteurs in the organization, that it was dangerous to ride in the elevators, that someone was tampering with his office locks, and that he was being poisoned. He began to hear strange and hostile voices that he incorrectly thought were coming from the office next door. His threat on the life of his boss finally brought him to the attention of mental health professionals.

Causes of Ralph's Disorder

What causes schizophrenia? No one knows for sure, but research studies indicate that the brains of schizophrenics are different from the brains of normal individuals. Schizophrenic brains are different in anatomical structure, electrophysiological function, and metabolism and in the concentration, structure, and functioning of neurotransmitters (Torrey, 1983). Data from family studies indicate that schizophrenia has a strong genetic component. Twin studies have shown a much higher concordance rate for monozygotic twins than for dizygotic twins. Adoption studies have shown that, in comparison with matched control groups, five times as many biological relatives of adopted schizophrenics had a schizophrenialike diagnosis. Over the years various psychological theories have been proposed to explain the causation of schizophrenia. Several point to pathological family interaction, with distorted and faulty family communication patterns. It has been theorized that the childhood environment may play a role in the development of major deficits in ego function, resulting in disturbances of thinking; difficulties with object-self differentiation; difficulties with intimate relationships; problems with attention, perception, cognition, and impulse control; and difficulty managing strong affects. It is clear that children growing up in a home in which one or more of the parents or close relatives are themselves seriously disturbed or schizophrenic will be at risk. Other theories of the causation of schizophrenia include nutritional theories, viral or infectious agent theories, theories of stress, theories about the mother-child bond, and sociocultural theories. Only further research and time will tell which of these theories is correct in explaining the development of schizophrenia.

Taken as a whole, the research data point to a number of risk factors in the development of schizophrenia: (1) a close relative who is schizophrenic; (2) a difficult obstetrical delivery with brain trauma; (3) difficulties in the early childhood environment, with disruption of normal psychosexual development; (4) a parent who is possessive, hostile, paranoid, or otherwise mentally disturbed; (5) low levels of monoamine oxidase B in blood platelets; (6) abnormal-pursuit eye movements; (7) drug use and abuse; and (8) a history of a specific neurological disorder, including temporal lobe epilepsy and Huntington's chorea.

What were the specific factors in Ralph's life that caused the development of schizophrenia? Ralph was probably predisposed to the development of schizophrenia due to genetic endowment from his father and possibly other relatives. In addition to the predisposing factors, Ralph had a number of precipitating factors that contributed to the onset of his most recent acute episode. First, Ralph's ingestion of amphetamines prior to his breakdown probably played a major role in the onset of this episode. Amphetamines and other classes of drugs can precipitate an acute schizophrenic episode. Second, the stresses of his job were a nonspecific stressor in the development of his disorder.

Psychological testing during the course of his most recent

hospitalization revealed that Ralph's reality testing was impaired and that he had only tenuous control over his impulses, behavior, and aggressive feelings. Ralph was unable to adequately modulate his emotions, so he tended to be swiftly overpowered by his intense aggressive feelings. His thinking at times was highly idiosyncratic, and his ego showed a looseness of boundaries and was fearful of being overwhelmed by powerful forces from within and without. Ralph had a strong tendency to project his aggressive impulses onto his auditory hallucinations in a way that made the world appear persecutory and menacing. This further heightened his sense of vulnerability, victimization, and anger. Ralph was also afraid he might act out some of his violent fantasies. In sum, Ralph was predisposed to the development of schizophrenia because of a genetic endowment that made him vulnerable to the development of schizophrenia. The precipitates of Ralph's acute schizophrenic episode appeared to be (1) the continuing and chronic effect of schizophrenia on the biological and psychological structures of his mind, (2) the use of amphetamines, and (3) the general stresses of the job.

What about the issue of Ralph's violence? How likely was it that Ralph would have actually physically harmed his boss? What are the probabilities that a schizophrenic senior executive will become violent and seriously injure or even kill her or his colleagues? In spite of the fact that stories about mentally ill persons who kill themselves, others, or both appear with some frequency in the national media, the mentally ill are less likely to engage in violence than the general population. Nevertheless, schizophrenia is the second-most-common diagnosis in mental patients who become violent (Kaplan and Sadock, 1985, p. 131). Fortunately, many mentally ill individuals are frightened of their violent thoughts or impulses and usually seek assistance to help themselves stay in control before they strike out. Individuals with a high risk of violence are largely those with a history of previous acts of violence, such as setting fires or abusing animals as a child, being victims of child abuse, collecting or using firearms, abusing drugs or alcohol, or having vengeful thoughts toward authority figures. However, even in the absence of these risk factors, it is impossible to rule out completely the possibility of violence in the mentally ill individual; thus, threats of physical harm must always be taken seriously.

Commonly Asked Questions About Schizophrenia and Executives

Question Number One Is schizophrenia any different in its onset, cause, appearance, or clinical course in senior executives than in other individuals with the disease? Senior executives are affected in the same way by schizophrenia as are other individuals. Because the disease often has a chronic, downhill course, schizophrenic senior executives who are still functioning in the corporate setting are usually in the early stages of the illness.

Question Number Two What is the relationship between stress that a senior executive may experience in the corporate setting and a predisposition to the development of schizophrenia? Stress alone cannot cause schizophrenia, not even in senior executives who may have a number of risk factors for development of the illness. In most instances stress can act as a nonspecific precipitant to the onset of the disease, but there is no agreed way to predict what stresses and level of intensity will cause a senior executive at risk to develop the disease.

Question Number Three If schizophrenia is so rare in senior executives and other professionals, why spend any time discussing it? It is true that schizophrenia is very uncommon in senior executives and others in upper socioeconomic circumstances. The reason why it is important to have an awareness and appreciation of the illness is that schizophrenic individuals in the acute phase of the illness, as stated above, are at risk of physical harm to themselves or others.

Question Number Four What is the difference between a "nervous breakdown" or a "psychotic break" and schizophrenia? The term *nervous breakdown* is frequently used by the lay public to describe what happens to an individual who, because of mental illness, however serious or benign, short lived or long term, becomes unable to function adequately in a social or occupational role. *Psychotic break* is a catchall clinical term used to describe what happens to an individual who experiences psychotic symptoms, that is, delusions and auditory or visual hallucinations for whatever reason. Only a certain percentage of individuals who experience a psychotic break will end up actually having schizophrenia.

Summary

Ralph was a paranoid schizophrenic whose illness significantly affected his business judgment and severely impaired his social and occupational functioning. Ralph's follow-up care as well as his overall treatment and prognosis will be discussed in a later chapter.

8

~~~~~~

Getting and Keeping
the Impaired Executive
in Treatment

Once a senior executive develops a problem with alcohol, illicit drugs, or mental illness, prompt and effective treatment is the next step. Because of the major advances made in the treatment of serious psychiatric illness in the last four decades, senior executives and others whose psychiatric illness is detected early and treated effectively stand the greatest chance of recovery with a rapid return to their jobs. But how does one determine when a senior executive is impaired enough to require medical attention and active intervention? What steps should one take to properly manage the senior executive who develops a problem with alcoholism, drug abuse, or mental illness? These and other questions about the management of the alcoholic, drug-abusing, or mentally ill senior executive will be answered in this chapter.

Determining That a Senior Executive Needs Treatment

Senior executives, like others who become psychiatrically impaired, are in an acute crisis situation resulting from (1) interpersonal conflict, (2) chemical abuse or dependency, (3) problems with work, (4) mourning and bereavement, (5) major life disasters, (6) reactions to personal assault or violence, (7) separation from familiar environments, or (8) suicidal ideation or attempt. The goal of all mental health treatment is the removal of acute symptoms and the stabilization of the individual's overall psychological and physical condition.

What are the specific behaviors that one should look for in the alcoholic, drug-addicted, or mentally ill senior executive? The behaviors of the five troubled executives whose stories were presented earlier are good examples of the types of behaviors that would warrant attention and require treatment intervention in any corporate setting. In review, intervention may be required for senior executives

- who become unpredictable and behave strangely and inappropriately
- who become easily overwhelmed and unable to manage intense and painful feelings, resulting in unpredictable and often violent emotional outbursts
- who become inappropriately aggressive or unexplainably withdrawn
- who become forgetful and lose track of flow and content of meetings
- who overreact to situations and lose their sense of humor or perspective
- who become suspicious and distrustful in their dealings with others in the firm
- who appear to lose touch with reality
- who become apathetic and pessimistic and lose their intellectual sharpness, political savvy, and good business sense
- who become indecisive and appear confused
- who lose all sense of perspective and misinterpret events in their environment
- who appear inappropriately intoxicated or hung over
- who have a large number of unexplained absences
- who appear tremulous, "shaky," and ill at ease

For example, it would be important to note if a poorly performing senior executive is frequently coming to work late, is complaining of headaches, is absent frequently on Mondays and Fridays, is taking longer than acceptable lunch breaks, and has the smell of alcohol on her or his breath during working hours. Another example would be a senior executive who, after becoming increasingly hostile, suspicious, and paranoid, inappropriately terminates key members of his or her staff.

Six Steps in Evaluation of an Impaired Executive

If you suspect that an underperforming senior executive is experiencing significant problems with alcoholism, drug abuse, or mental illness, there are a number of specific steps to take.

Step One: Collect as Many Data as Possible   Collect as many data from as many sources as possible that confirm that the troubled senior executive's job performance and overall occupational functioning have significantly declined. This is particularly important to ensure objectivity and also to protect against possible future litigation by the senior executive in question. Good sources of data include the troubled executive's colleagues, senior personnel executives who may have had contact with the troubled executive, and one's own observations. In a confidential file write the time, date, and nature of all inappropriate, bizarre, or out-of-character behaviors and their probable impact on the troubled executive's job performance. Be discreet; avoid the appearance of a witch-hunt. Do not depend on hearsay, rumors, and back-room gossip. Be aware of individuals who may have ulterior motives for providing negative information about the executive in question.

If there is not time to personally collect the relevant data, then assign a senior member of the personnel staff in whom you have confidence. As the data are being collected, do not jump to conclusions or try to make premature decisions. No single behavior is conclusive for the presence of alcoholism, drug abuse, or major mental illness. Keep an open mind and give the senior executive the benefit of the doubt. The time frame for collecting the data is different in each case, but if the symptoms are serious, data collection should take no more than a few weeks. What happens if the senior executive learns that confidential data about him or her are being collected and demands an explanation? Be straightforward and tell the senior executive the truth, that is, that there is concern about his or her recent job performance and behavior, and data are being collected from a variety of sources in an attempt to make an objective evaluation.

Step Two: Analyze the Data   After the data have been collected, review all the information in detail. Two questions should be asked. Is the troubled senior executive showing a significant decline in job performance? Is the executive's deteriorating job performance most likely a consequence of an emotional, psychological, or substance-abuse problem? If the answer to these questions is no, go no further. If the answer to both questions is yes, you can comfortably proceed with a plan of intervention. If, however, the senior executive appears to be performing in a competent to outstanding manner but still appears to be experiencing some "personal difficulties," it makes good sense to leave well enough alone. Senior executives who develop major and enduring problems with alcoholism, drug abuse, or mental illness will soon exhibit significant deterioration in their job performance, signaling appropriate intervention by others in the firm. Otherwise, if the job performance of the senior executive in question "isn't broke, don't fix it."

Step Three: Meet with Other Colleagues to Review the Data   Once the two questions have been answered to your satisfaction, meet with a trusted and experienced colleague, preferably the senior executive responsible for personnel and human resources, to review all the data, including your own conclusions. This will ensure greater objectivity by minimizing the injection of personal bias into the conclusions about the troubled executive's job performance and overall emotional and psychological well-being.

Step Four: Consult with a Mental Health Consultant   Once the senior personnel executive and you agree that the senior executive in question is exhibiting significant problems with his or her job performance that seem to be a consequence of alcoholism, drug abuse, or mental illness, then an outside mental health consultant should be called in to make a formal assessment. The consultant will review the collected data and determine whether the executive in question appears to be having significant psychological difficulties. If the mental health professional does not agree with you that the senior executive is having a problem, the matter should be dropped. If, however, the consultant concludes that the executive is having serious difficulties with alcoholism, drug abuse, or mental illness, then he or she will recommend that the executive undergo a one-to-two-hour mental health assessment.

Step Five: Meet with the Troubled Senior Executive After meeting with the mental health consultant, schedule a short meeting (no more than thirty minutes) with the troubled senior executive. The participants in the meeting should include yourself, the senior personnel executive, and the troubled executive. It is better not to discuss your findings and thoughts with the troubled executive over the telephone. Simply say that the agenda of the proposed meeting will be to review "how things are going."

Begin the meeting by asking the troubled senior executive for his or her opinion about how things have been going on the job. Once the executive begins speaking, notice any unusual, out-of-character, or inappropriate speech patterns. Pay attention to the flow, logic, and coherence of his or her thinking. Watch for any unnecessary defensiveness or inappropriate emotional outbursts. After the executive has finished speaking, review the data that support the findings of deteriorating job performance. Be clear, direct, and to the point. If you make a strong case in the interview, the executive will usually agree with the assessment and exhibit an interest in getting some help for his or her problem. At this point, recommend that the executive undergo a short evaluation by the mental health consultant to determine what to do next.

Unfortunately, in some cases the presentation of the findings is met with vehement and energetic denials. The troubled senior executive may accuse "others" in the firm of "spreading malicious lies and rumors" in order to tarnish his or her reputation and destroy his or her career. Stay calm. Do not argue, become defensive, or threaten. Instead, state that you have listened to the executive's position and that there is clearly a difference in opinions about how he or she is doing. Calmly repeat that there is clear documentation of significant job deterioration, and that if job performance does not improve quickly and substantially, appropriate disciplinary action will be taken up to and including possible dismissal. Most resistent troubled senior executives, when confronted with disciplinary action and the possible loss of employment, will submit to an evaluation by the mental health consultant.

Step Six: Arrange a Mental Health Evaluation of the Troubled Senior Executive An appointment should be made through your office to have the troubled senior executive evaluated by the mental health consultant at an off-site location; the evaluation should be paid for by the firm. At the beginning of the examination the troubled senior executive will sign a release-of-information statement, legally allowing the mental health consultant to communicate directly with you and the senior personnel executive about findings and recommendations. Near the end of the evaluation, the mental health consultant will also present his or her findings and recommendations for treatment directly to the troubled senior executive.

Pretreatment Meeting

Once you have received and reviewed the findings and treatment recommendations resulting from the mental health consultant's evaluation of the troubled senior executive, you, the senior personnel officer, and the mental health consultant should schedule a final pretreatment meeting with the troubled executive to discuss and agree on a number of important issues. This meeting is important to ensure the impaired executive's cooperation and to decrease the chance of his or her prematurely terminating the recommended treatment process.

Issue One: Length of Stay The decision to agree to the recommendation for treatment, particularly within the setting of an inpatient mental health facility, is often a difficult one.

The impaired senior executive may be unsure or frightened of the idea of being confined for a significant period of time. The mental health consultant should reassure the executive that the length of stay for an acute psychiatric hospitalization is relatively short. Hospitalization may last anywhere from several days to several months, depending on the nature of the problem, the success of the treatments, and the overall progress of the executive. During the past ten years the average length of hospitalization has been declining across the country; stays of thirty days or less are increasingly the norm.

Issue Two: Violence in the Hospital Setting An impaired senior executive may wonder whether fellow patients at the institution can be kept under adequate control by the staff so that there is no threat of physical assault or violence. The mental health consultant should make it clear that the physical safety of all patients is assured at all times by a highly trained and competent staff. Violent, out-of-control patients make up only a very small percentage of the typical inpatient psychiatric population at the average private psychiatric facility.

Issue Three: Usefulness of Treatment The impaired senior executive may also worry about whether the hospital stay will be useful, or whether being surrounded by other mentally unstable individuals may simply aggravate the illness. He or she should understand that the inpatient facility provides a supportive, safe, and controlled environment that provides for optimum opportunities for extensive evaluation and treatment. The mental health consultant should state that the vast majority of patients admitted to psychiatric facilities benefit from the experience. There is no evidence that being surrounded by other patients with similar problems hinders one's recovery. Quite the contrary—the support that a patient receives from other patients is an important part of the treatment process.

Issue Four: Nature of the Admission Process The senior executive should be informed that, once admitted, he or she and his or her family are interviewed in the admissions office, the appropriate paperwork is filled out, and the appropriate forms are signed by the patient or the responsible guardian. Then the executive is escorted to the unit where his or her luggage is checked for prohibited items, including sharp objects and unauthorized medication. The executive is given a tour of the unit, introduced to the other patients, and briefed on the unit's rules and regulations. The executive is then seen for separate psychiatric evaluations by the nursing staff and by the attending psychiatrist. The executive also receives a complete physical examination and history by the consulting physician or other appropriate medical doctor. A preliminary treatment plan is developed, and the executive formally begins his or her treatment program.

Issue Five: Types of Treatment   Therapies for the senior executive may include individual insight-oriented psychotherapy, family therapy, short-term psychotherapy, group psychotherapy, behavioral therapy, activity therapy, and medication therapy. The mental health consultant should inform the executive that the day-to-day schedule is usually very full, with meetings and therapy sessions. Individual psychotherapy or hospital visits by the psychiatrist occur usually three to seven times a week. The executive usually has group therapy about three times a week. Family therapy with the executive and his or her family occurs once or twice a week. Community meetings, group counseling, and individual meetings with other members of the professional staff may occur daily. In addition, the executive will be assigned to groups involved in occupational therapy, recreational therapy, leisure counseling, art therapy, and medication therapy. The executive is usually up by 7:00 A.M. and asleep by 10:00 P.M. Because of the intensity of the treatment program, the executive's family is restricted to specific visiting hours—usually several hours in the evenings and on weekends. Units differ with regard to their attitude toward passes home during hospitalization. As a general rule, home passes are restricted until the executive has demonstrated that his or her clinical condition has stabilized. The decision to issue a pass is usually made jointly by the staff and the psychiatrist, with input from the other patients and from the executive's family.

The individual's psychiatrist is in charge of the treatment

team, which is made up of the above-mentioned mental health professionals. The treatment team usually meets regularly to review the treatment progress and to make modifications and adjustments as necessary. Although all decisions are made by the treatment team as a group, the psychiatrist is ultimately responsible, both legally and medically, for the patient and has the final say.

Issue Six: The Decision of Discharge   The impaired senior executive may also be concerned about whether he or she will be allowed to return home when he or she feels ready. The mental health consultant should communicate to the troubled executive that the decision to discharge is one that is made jointly by the treatment team, the psychiatrist, the patient, and the patient's family. After treatment, most patients feel that the length of their stay was appropriate to the needs of their recovery. Many impaired senior executives are concerned about the possible negative impact their hospitalization will have on their careers when they return to work. The impaired executive should be reassured by the senior personnel executive that he or she will have the full support of the firm during this period of recovery and that every effort will be made to reintegrate her or him into the firm. Finally, the senior executive needs to be reassured that the cost of treatment will not put a strain on the executive's financial resources. The senior personnel officer should explain to the executive that the company's comprehensive group health insurance policy will pay for the bulk of the cost of treatment.

Other issues to be covered during this final pretreatment meeting should include (1) mechanisms for salary support, including short-term disability and sick leave during the executive's absence; (2) designation of other executives in the firm to handle the executive's responsibilities during his or her absence; and (3) types and frequency of contact between the troubled executive, the treating professionals, and the senior personnel executives during the course of treatment. Once the above information has been communicated to the senior executive, he or she is then ready to be admitted to the inpatient mental health facility.

Keeping the Impaired Executive in Treatment

Once the executive enters treatment, how do you ensure that he or she stays in treatment and progresses satisfactorily? First, it is important that a senior personnel executive be in weekly contact with both the executive who is undergoing treatment and with the treating professionals to get an update on how the treatment is progressing. When the executive begins treatment, he or she will sign a release statement allowing the personnel executive to be updated weekly. Second, prior to the beginning of treatment, the troubled executive will clearly understand that there will be two major conditions under which he or she will be allowed to return to work: (1) satisfactory completion of the treatment as recommended and documented by the treating professionals and (2) agreement by the executive to abide by the recommendations of the treating professionals for ongoing and appropriate aftercare.

What to Do If the Executive Is in an Acute Crisis

What about the case of the senior executive who goes into an acute crisis because of alcoholism, drug abuse, or mental illness, requiring immediate intervention? In a minority of cases there will be no time to collect and review data. The troubled executive is in acute crisis, and immediate action has to be taken. What is the definition of the executive in acute crisis? Individuals who need immediate attention include

- those who are acutely suicidal or threatening suicide
- those who are acutely homicidal or threatening homicide
- those who clearly have lost touch with reality due to delusional thinking or auditory or visual hallucinations
- those who are acutely and severely intoxicated and unable to function minimally
- those who are experiencing withdrawal from alcohol or other drugs with possible seizures

Under these circumstances the senior executive should immediately be seen by you or the senior personnel executive to confirm that he or she needs immediate help. If the senior executive understands that he is in acute crisis and agrees to immediate help, then a nearby mental health facility should be contacted and the patient rushed by ambulance to the facility that day.

In a minority of cases of acute illness, the senior executive in question either will not be fully aware of the seriousness of his or her condition or will vehemently deny that he or she is having a problem, much less agree to seek treatment in an inpatient facility. What do you do? You seek involuntary commitment to a mental health facility. The temporary involuntary commitment process is governed by the laws of each state. Although the involuntary commitment process in many states has been abused over the years, in the past decade or so the process has been modified to protect the rights of patients as well as those of society.

There are two basic stages to the commitment process, and two types of commitment: emergency and long term. Emergency involuntary commitment is usually for no more than seventy-two hours and in many states can be initiated by any concerned individual such as you, the senior personnel officer, family members, the police, and mental health professionals. An evaluation by a psychiatrist may not be required prior to detaining the individual. After the senior executive refuses to voluntarily seek treatment in a mental health facility, contact the police, requesting an emergency involuntary commitment for the executive in question. The police will arrive and escort her or him to the proper facility, and an emergency involuntary commitment order will be signed by the local magistrate.

During the seventy-two hours the detained executive is required by court order to undergo a psychiatric evaluation by a licensed psychiatrist, who later presents his findings in one or two hearings before a judge. The executive is allowed to attend the hearing and may be represented by legal counsel. After hearing the testimony of the psychiatrist, the executive, and other interested parties, the judge makes a determination as to whether the executive requires further psychiatric care. If the decision is in the affirmative, the executive will be committed to a local psychiatric facility for a specified period of time. If, however, the judge decides that the executive's condition does not warrant further inpatient psychiatric care, she or he is released on her or his own recognizance.

Summary

There are a number of steps to take to successfully manage the troubled senior executive one suspects of having a problem with alcoholism, drug abuse, or mental illness. These steps include collecting and analyzing appropriate data, conferring with colleagues, meeting with the troubled executive, arranging a mental health evaluation, and arranging a pretreatment meeting with the troubled executive. In rare cases the acuteness of the executive's emerging problem will not allow time for following a step-by-step plan. Under these circumstances specific actions to initiate treatment must be taken immediately. Once the troubled executive is in treatment, there are specific things to do that will ensure that he or she stays in treatment until it is completed.

9

~~~~~~

Managing the Recovering
Executive's Return
to Work

Successfully managing the recovering senior executive's return requires careful planning, coordination, and follow-up. The key to the successful reentry of a recovered executive into the firm is an appropriate aftercare plan. Planning for aftercare should begin while the executive is still in the hospital. Members of the aftercare planning group should include the recovering senior executive, the executive's family, the treating inpatient mental health professionals, the firm's mental health consultant, and the senior personnel officer. Keep in mind that the returning senior executive is still in a state of recovery and will only gradually regain his or her former level of productivity and effectiveness. Powers of concentration, memory, energy level, and overall analytical capacities will all be recovered slowly. The senior executive taking prescribed psychotropic medication may be still adjusting to the side effects of the medication, including drowsiness and decreased alertness. In addition, follow-up appointments for outpatient therapy and attendance at AA, NA, or other self-help group meetings will limit his or her availability. If the recovering senior executive's reentry into the corporate work environment is too abrupt—trying to play catch-up too quickly—there is an increased risk of a relapse.

Common Concerns About the Recovering Executive's
Return to Work

What are some common concerns about the recovering senior executive's returning to work after a stay in an inpatient mental health facility?

Concern Number One   What should I say to the recovering executive's peers and subordinates about his or her whereabouts during treatment when he or she returns to the firm? Because of the importance of confidentiality, little should be said about the whereabouts or the nature of the problem of the troubled senior executive during the period of inpatient treatment. Once the executive returns to work, he or she should be encouraged to meet with the key staff and immediate subordinates to explain that (1) he or she has been under the care of health professionals, (2) things are much better, (3) he or she will be gradually reintegrating into the work routines, and (4) he or she will need the help and support of everyone to make the recovery a success. Of course, the recovering senior executive is under no obligation to say anything to anyone about the details of treatment or recovery. But total silence by the recovering senior executive often fuels rumors and heightens unspoken staff concerns that are probably better dealt with if the recovering senior executive is somewhat open with the staff.

Concern Number Two   Is there something that might inadvertently precipitate a relapse in the recovering executive? The answer is no. Many supervisors are anxious about doing anything that might harm the chances of the returning executive's recovering fully. As a consequence, they might be inclined to treat the executive delicately. It is important to maintain the usual supervisory relationship. Do not be afraid. Be clear, communicate frequently, have appropriate expectations, set limits, and give appropriate feedback. Should you try to avoid the topic of the recovering senior executive's illness, treatment, and ongoing recovery and behave as if nothing had happened? The answer is no. Be interested, cordial, and open. Follow the lead of the recovering senior executive. Do not pretend that nothing has happened. Also do not pretend that a relapse is not possible. Encourage the senior executive to have one-on-one meetings with the other executives and staff to get support, advice, and encouragement. Encourage the returning executive to convene meetings with staff to discuss their fears, concerns, and worries.

Concern Number Three *Should I behave like a counselor and have discussions with the recovering executive about his or her personal issues?* The answer is no. Leave the treatment up to the aftercare treatment team. Do not try to become the recovering executive's psychotherapist.

Steps to Take in Managing the Recovering Executive

There are a number of steps to take to successfully manage the recovering senior executive's return to work.

Step One *Meet with the Senior Executive During the Treatment Phase.* Meet with the recovering senior executive while he or she is still in the hospital and confer with the treatment staff in order to get a sense of the executive's progress during treatment. Be supportive of his or her treatment and recovery. Take advantage of any educational programs on alcoholism, drug abuse, and mental illness offered in the inpatient mental health facility, including those presented by Alcoholics Anonymous and Narcotics Anonymous.

Step Two *Meet with the Aftercare Planning Group.* Meet with the recovering executive and the other members of the aftercare planning group to discuss and plan an individualized and appropriate aftercare treatment plan. A good aftercare plan will have a number of components, depending on the needs of the recovering executive, including (1) outpatient psychotherapy, (2) medication therapy, (3) outpatient treatment or support for chemical dependency and abuse, (4) support services for the senior executive's family, and (5) appropriate changes in the senior executive's job circumstances and responsibilities.

Step Three   Meet with the Recovering Senior Executive. Meet with the recovering senior executive and put together a plan for reduced activities and responsibilities once she or he returns to work. After discharge the executive will need to be gradually reintegrated into her or his work environment. The process of reintegration may require temporary or permanent changes in the recovering executive's work routines and job responsibilities. The recovering executive should return to work only on a half-time basis for the first two to four weeks. Either while the executive is still in the inpatient mental health treatment facility or immediately after discharge, the recovering senior executive's superiors should meet with her or him to determine what important projects or other activities were not accomplished or completed during her or his absence. Then a priority list of projects and a time frame for accomplishing the assignments should be developed. The guiding principle for the development of the priority list and the time frame should be to avoid overburdening the recovering senior executive with a large number of urgent tasks and demands.

Step Four   Plan for the Possibility of Relapse. Meet with the recovering senior executive and several members of the aftercare treatment team to plan for the possibility of relapse. Outline the steps that must be taken should the recovering executive begin to exhibit a recurrence of the signs and symptoms of emotional dysfunction and declining work performance. These steps should include (1) reexamination by the mental health consultant, (2) discussion with the aftercare treatment team, and (3) discussion with the senior executive in question.

Step Five   Convene Periodic Meetings. Convene periodic meetings with the recovering senior executive, his or her boss, the outpatient treating professionals, the senior personnel executive, and the mental health consultant. These meetings will serve several purposes, including monitoring the rate of recovery and the recovering executive's job performance.

What about the issue of travel? The rule of thumb is that all travel for the first several months at least should be significantly curtailed. Air travel across time zones should be particularly avoided. Travel places a significant physical and mental strain on the recovering executive. In addition, long trips interfere with the recovering executive's ability to attend the important aftercare therapies and self-help group meetings that are so crucial for complete recovery.

Aftercare Planning for the Alcoholic or Drug-Dependent Executive

Aftercare planning for the alcoholic or drug-dependent individual involves the scheduling and coordination of a variety of treatment activities. Recovering alcoholics or drug abusers have the highest chance of recovery when two or more of these aftercare treatment modalities are used in combination. These treatment activities and services may include outpatient psychotherapy, family and couples therapy, Alcoholics Anonymous (AA) meetings, Al-Anon meetings, Narcotics Anonymous (NA) meetings, Adult Children of Alcoholics meetings, and medication therapy.

Alcoholics Anonymous is a self-help voluntary organization composed of recovering alcoholic men and women. The organization was begun in 1935 by a stockbroker and a surgeon, both of whom were alcoholics. Through a unique twelve-step program, AA assists recovering alcoholics in maintaining sobriety, regaining self-esteem, and rebuilding their lives. Al-Anon, Narcotics Anonymous, and Adult Children of Alcoholics are also self-help voluntary organizations patterned along the same lines as AA. Recovering alcoholics are usually required to attend an AA or NA meeting daily for the first thirty to ninety days after discharge. For the recovering senior executive whose work schedule is heavy and who may have significant travel commitments, attending a large number of meetings may be difficult. Nevertheless, attendance at these meetings is crucial because this is where he or she will get the majority of his or her support for staying sober. The recovering executive may also experience difficulty talking about him- or herself in front of a large group of strangers. Fortunately, it gets easier with attendance at subsequent meetings. Recovering senior executives may also feel uncomfortable realizing that many individuals in the meetings are from different social, educational, and occupational strata. Fortunately, over time the common denominator of alcoholism or drug dependency provides the glue for many lasting relationships.

Support Services for the Executive's Family

The families of recovering senior executives are often in need of support services to help them cope with the recovering executive's problems. One important option is family therapy, which is an outpatient treatment for families that are experiencing significant stress and tension. The family meets with the psychotherapist for sixty to ninety minutes per session. The goal of the treatment is to observe, identify, and understand the maladaptive interactions and miscommunications among family members. During sessions the family members have an opportunity to express their views about the nature and origin of their problems. With the family therapist's assistance, families gain insight into their pathological ways of interacting and seek to change these maladaptive patterns with new skills of communication and interaction.

Another option for the recovering senior executive's spouse is marital or couples therapy, which is specifically designed for couples who are experiencing significant problems with their relationships. Common areas of conflict include sex, finances, children, and in-laws. The treatment seeks to assist each partner in understanding the dynamics of the other as it impacts on their relationship. The goal of the treatment is to increase communications, resolve conflicts, foster greater understanding and empathy of the other partner's positions and feelings, and learn more adaptive patterns of behavior. Treatment can last from several months to several years, depending on the nature of the problem, and the financial cost per session is moderate. This treatment is useful for the recovering senior executive's family or spouse, who may be experiencing significant problems for whatever reason. The senior executive with a highly authoritarian style with one-way communication may find these treatments trying in the beginning but eventually useful.

The third option is Al-Anon—a self-help voluntary organization patterned along the lines of AA. Al-Anon is a support organization whose goal is to provide education and support for the spouses of recovering alcoholics.

What If the Executive Relapses?

Unfortunately, relapse is a reality for anyone who has been acutely afflicted with major mental illness or a significant drug or alcohol problem. As mentioned in an earlier chapter, there is no cure for these disorders, making the possibility of relapse and future acute illness a distinct possibility. Recovering senior executives or others who have been treated for mental illness or a serious drug or alcohol problem may relapse for several reasons. First, after discharge they may feel sufficiently recovered that they may lose their motivation to attend required aftercare therapies and treatment meetings. They may feel that the time and energy involved in pursuing their aftercare treatments are not worth the payback. They become caught up in the day-to-day demands of the office and begin missing meetings and therapy sessions. Unfortunately, many recovering individuals significantly underestimate their own fragility after discharge, which only becomes obvious in hindsight after their first relapse.

The second and perhaps the most common cause of relapse is discontinuation by the recovering individual of prescribed psychiatric medication. As described earlier, the major psychiatric medications are associated with significant side effects that may be uncomfortable or irritating. They cause frequent complaints of tremors, fatigue, weight gain, decreased mental acuity, and increased urination, to name a few. Research continues on the development of new medications with fewer side effects, but progress is slow. For recovering individuals who feel "well," the temptation to discontinue their medication without authorization by their treating professionals is great.

Discontinuing medication without authorization almost invariably leads to relapse.

A major cause of relapse for recovering drug abusers or alcoholics is resumption of the use of drugs or alcohol. Recovering drug abusers or alcoholics will not infrequently have a great deal of trouble, particularly in the early phases of their illness, believing that they cannot "do drugs" or "take a drink" occasionally without serious consequences. They cannot. One drink invariably leads to another. Major mental illness, drug addiction, and alcoholism are long-term, chronic, remitting illnesses.

Even the best aftercare program religiously followed by the recovering senior executive will not guarantee a relapse-free recovery. The best preparation for the possibility of relapse in the recovering senior executive is to hope for the best but be prepared for the worst. The best one can do is ensure that the recovering senior executive stays involved with the aftercare treatment program. Major deviations from the plan will without question result in a higher risk of relapse. Also, the role of the recovering executive's family becomes pivotal in providing additional oversight and in encouraging the recovering executive to follow the aftercare treatment plan. Family support can often make the difference between success and failure in the individual's long-term recovery.

What If the Executive Cannot Return to Work?

Even after an intensive inpatient treatment experience, there will always be some individuals who, because of the continuing debilitating effect of their illness, will not be able to return to work. For example, individuals whose long-term alcohol or drug abuse has resulted in significant physical damage, such as intractable liver disease or brain damage, may be unable to work. Chronic schizophrenics or individuals with poorly controlled bipolar illness are other examples. What happens to these individuals? In most cases they are forced to retire prematurely on medical disability. For many senior executives, private disability insurance is available either on an individual basis or through their employer. There are usually two types of disability programs—short term and long term. Short-term disability insurance is usually limited to fifty-two weeks and provides income support for the senior executive during his or her hospitalization and aftercare. Long-term disability is for the senior executive who is considered permanently disabled. The waiting period for many of these plans is several months after other short-term disability has been exhausted. Unfortunately, it is not uncommon for individuals who are forced to permanently retire on medical disability to do poorly in terms of life satisfaction. Inactivity, loss of sense of purpose, and lack of a daily structured activity also greatly aggravate their alcoholism, drug addiction, or mental illness. These individuals usually do better if they are engaged in some kind of structured daily activity.

When to Dismiss the Impaired Executive

It is always difficult to decide when one should "cut one's losses" and terminate the alcoholic, drug-abusing, or mentally ill senior executive. A useful corporate policy is to guarantee that all troubled senior executives, no matter how impaired, are entitled to at least one opportunity to receive treatment for their disorder without prejudice to their current job or their future career prospects. Should the recovering executive, after a reasonable period of time (as defined by the aftercare clinicians and the mental health consultant), continue to function below expectations even with the support of a well-structured aftercare program, then the possibility of retirement on medical disability or outright discharge should be entertained. From a legal-liability point of view, it is critical that any eventual termination from the firm be solely a result of inability to satisfactorily perform the responsibilities of the job. The recovering executive needs to be given every chance to improve his or her performance. Lateral job transfer, a downgrading of job responsibilities, or an outright demotion are important options to consider before disability retirement or outright discharge. It is very important to avoid the appearance of discrimination by not discharging the recovering senior executive for reasons other than those that are strictly job related. Be sure to document all attempts to reintegrate the recovering senior executive into the firm. Remember that wrongful-discharge suits are, in this litigious society, an increasingly common phenomenon.

What about the impaired senior executive who either refuses the initial treatment recommendations or, after hospitalization, refuses to cooperate with the aftercare treatment team? Can he or she be summarily dismissed? It is important to check with the firm's legal counsel, but the conservative answer is probably no. It is entirely within a person's right to refuse treatment. It is not uncommon to be confronted with the recalcitrant senior executive who is clearly impaired and who refuses help but who continues to perform adequately, if minimally. What should one do in this situation? Wait and hope that the executive in question will eventually resign, ask for help, or perform poorly enough to allow one to take action.

Summary

There are three keys to the successful postdischarge recovery of an alcoholic, drug-addicted, or mentally ill senior executive. First, an appropriate and successful aftercare plan involving a number of significant players, including the recovering executive, the executive's family, the executive's superiors at work, and the outpatient mental health treatment professionals, must be developed. Second, the aftercare treatment plan must be a diversified one that includes a number of different outpatient treatments and support services, including outpatient psychotherapy, counseling, self-help groups, family support services, and psychotropic medications. Last of all, temporary adjustments must be made in the recovering executive's job responsibilities and activities to accommodate aftercare treatment activities and to allow her or him to slowly ease back into job routines.

10

~~~~~~

Developing a Corporate
Policy for Dealing with
Impaired Executives

The Why, What, Where, and for Whom of Corporate Policy

A crucial component of any successful organizational strategy that addresses the issue of the impaired senior executive is a clear description of the firm's philosophy, policy, and procedures for the impaired executive. The company policy must specifically address the issues of why, what, where, and for whom.

What are the whys of a company policy for the impaired senior executive? In its introduction the company policy statement should reflect four major beliefs. The first belief is that outstanding senior executive performance is crucial to the firm's long-term prosperity and that experienced, loyal, and productive senior executives are the firm's most important strategic asset. The second belief is that alcoholism, drug abuse, and mental illness are diseases, and like physical illnesses are beyond the executive's control, that can strike down the most capable and able executive, rather than being viewed as evidence of willful misconduct or moral weakness. The third belief is that because senior executive performance is significantly impaired by drugs, alcohol, and mental illness, any delay in taking prompt and appropriate action is not appropriate. The fourth and last major belief is that in order to avoid long-term senior executive disability and eventual separation from the firm, all senior xecutives must make it their responsibility to act promptly to help an impaired colleague so that these impaired senior executives can be treated, recover quickly from their illnesses, and return to work fully recovered.

In terms of the question of for whom, the policy should clearly state that this is a new company policy and program that will focus exclusively on the problem of the impaired senior executive. The definition of senior executive will differ from organization to organization but will generally include all individuals in the firm who possess broad, senior, and substantial responsibility. In a firm with many divisions and subsidiaries, usually the top management of the major divisions are included in the definition of senior management. The problem of the troubled employee, supervisory manager, and middle manager must be dealt with in a separate program. If the firm already has a functioning employee-assistance program (EAP) for employees and lower-level managers, refer to the company EAP policy as a guide for developing a policy for the impaired senior executive. The firm's EAP policies and policies on the impaired senior executive will contain many similarities, and EAP counselors are a useful resource when drafting the initial company policy on the troubled senior executive. One may legitimately ask the question, at this point, "Are two separate and distinct company policies and programs—one for the employees and lower-level managers and one for the senior managers, really necessary in this age of restructuring and streamlining operations?" Unfortunately, yes. As mentioned in Chapter One, senior executives are often reluctant, for a variety of reasons, to use services that were originally designed for employees, supervisory management, or middle management. A separate and distinct policy and set of procedures for the impaired senior executive are more likely to ensure that the unique problems, issues, and needs of the impaired senior executive are addressed.

It is important for the new company policy to describe where the program will be located in the corporate structure. Given the crucial importance of the firm's senior personnel officer in this new program, it should formally be located in his or her office. Even if the firm has a number of large, geographically dispersed divisions and subsidiaries, it is still important for the office of the senior corporate personnel officer to be the locus of the program. Because the senior corporate personnel officer either outranks or is at least on a level with many other senior executives in the organization, his or her recommendations and decisions about a given impaired senior executive will carry the most weight. In addition, it is important for the mental health consultant to work with and report directly to the most senior personnel officer of the company in order to ensure that the consultant's recommendations are given support from the highest levels of the organization. This will ensure more rapid decision making and less delay in the referral, treatment, and reintegration of the impaired and recovering senior executive.

Finally, the policy statement should describe in detail the whats of the proposed program. The essential components of a program for the impaired senior executive have been described in previous chapters. In review, the core components are commitment of the senior management to the new company policy, early detection of impaired performance and behavior that may be caused by mental illness or alcohol or drug abuse, documentation and reporting of such behavior to the senior personnel officer or by other executives, review of the collected data by the senior personnel executive in conjunction with the mental health consultant, confrontation of the impaired senior executive, referral and follow-up of treatment in a mental health facility, and reintegration of the treated and recovering senior executive into the firm.

It must be made clear in the policy statement that all senior executives are strongly encouraged to monitor their own performance and voluntarily seek help from their supervisor and senior personnel officer when they suspect they are developing a problem with alcohol, drug abuse, or mental illness. The executive, as supervisor, should monitor, evaluate, and document job performance of the executives he or she supervises and report to the senior personnel officer any evidence of diminished executive performance that might be caused by drug abuse, alcoholism, or mental illness. It is important for the supervising executive to refrain from jumping to conclusions, talking to the executive in question directly, or talking to other executives about the executive in question—assessment, confrontation, and treatment referral are the job of the senior personnel executive and the mental health consultant.

The policy should also state that the role of the senior personnel executive is to advocate the use of the program by all senior executives; oversee executive education and training; constantly upgrade his or her own level of knowledge of executive alcoholism, drug abuse, and mental illness; assess, confront, and refer for treatment the impaired senior executive; monitor the impaired executive's treatment; assist the recovering executive reintegrate into the firm; and periodically evaluate the impact of the new company policy.

A very important part of any company program and policy is the issue of confidentiality. It must be made very clear in the company policy statement that confidentiality is a crucial part of the program and that every effort will be made to maintain the confidentiality of the impaired senior executive. There are several important components to the issue of confidentiality. First, the impaired senior executive's records will not be part of the executive's regular personnel file; rather, such records will be held in a separate file by the mental health consultant, preferably off the company's premises. Second, professional ethics requires that the mental health consultant and treating mental health professionals hold all information obtained from the patient in evaluations and treatments in confidence. In the absence of a subpoena, the mental health professional in most cases is under no legal obligation to reveal any confidential information about the patient to outside parties, including the police. State laws and their interpretations are in constant flux with regard to the issue of threats to the well-being of others made by the patient in the presence of the psychiatrist.

It is important that the senior personnel executive be very familiar with current legal positions on this issue in her or his state. In most cases the senior executive who is undergoing evaluation or treatment will sign a release statement allowing the mental health consultant and the treating mental health professionals to release information about his or her condition. But it is important to realize that the executive is acting entirely within his or her legal rights if he or she refuses to sign a release-of-information statement. Under those circumstances the laws in most states will protect the patient's psychiatric records from unauthorized distribution.

Example of Corporate Policy for the Impaired Executive

I have described the essential elements of a good corporate policy for impaired senior executives. The following sections provide an example of a corporate policy on the impaired senior executive that contains all the essential elements.

Introduction and Program Philosophy

Optimal performance by all senior executives is crucial to the firm's long-term prosperity. Experienced and productive senior executives are the firm's most important strategic asset. The company recognizes that a senior executive who experiences mild to moderate personal problems may successfully deal with these problems independently and privately, resulting in little if any adverse impact on his or her job performance. However, alcoholism, drug abuse, and mental illness are diseases that, like physical illnesses, can strike down the most capable and able senior executive. Any delay in taking prompt and appropriate action can result in eventual loss of the executive with severe deterioration or death. In order to avoid long-term senior executive disability and eventual separation from the firm, all senior executives must now make it their responsibility to act promptly to help an impaired senior colleague so that he or she can be treated, recover quickly from the illness, and return to work fully recovered. For the purposes of this program a "senior executive" will be defined as anyone in the organization who possesses broad, senior, and substantial responsibility. This program is in addition to, and wholly separate from, all current firm activities or programs providing assistance to the troubled employee, supervisory manager, or middle manager.

Program Location and Office of Responsibility

The program will be located within the office of the senior corporate personnel officer, who will have complete responsibility for the program and its operation. The senior corporate personnel officer will be assisted in her or his duties by the corporate mental health consultant and others, as designated.

Program Procedures and Operation

Senior executives are strongly encouraged to monitor their own performance and voluntarily seek help from the company's senior personnel officer when they suspect they are developing a problem with alcohol, drug abuse, or mental illness. If a senior executive is exhibiting the signs and symptoms of alcoholism, drug abuse, or major mental illness; is experiencing a deterioration of job performance; and is unwilling or unable to seek help, then the immediate superior of the senior executive in question should notify the company's senior personnel officer. Data concerning the impaired senior executive's psychological status and job performance should be reviewed. If the data warrant, a referral for a more extensive evaluation by the firm's mental health consultant will be made. It is the responsibility of every senior executive to comply with the referral to the mental health consultant. If, in the opinion of the mental health consultant, further evaluation and treatment are called for, it is the responsibility of the senior executive in question to comply with all treatment recommendations. All impaired senior executives will receive prompt and appropriate treatment for their problems with alcoholism, drug abuse, or mental illness and will be assured that their job will not be threatened because of their decision to accept treatment for their condition. Release from one's job responsibilities will be granted during the course of treatment. The impaired executive may be entitled to sick-leave pay and/or short-term disability payments consistent with his or her employment contract and benefits. The recovering executive will be assisted by the mental health consultant and the senior personnel officer in reintegrating into the firm once his or her off-site treatment has been completed. The impaired executive's refusal to utilize the company's assistance will not be grounds for dismissal, but the impaired executive will be made aware that if his or her job performance continues to deteriorate, he or she will be subject to the usual disciplinary actions. Under no circumstances will the company's program for the impaired executive be used as a covert means to discipline or dismiss an executive.

Confidentiality

All treatment and medical records will be confidential, and every effort will be made to maintain the confidentiality of the impaired senior executive. The impaired senior executive's records will not be part of his or her regular personnel file; such records will be held in a separate file by the mental health consultant, preferably off the company's premises. The mental health consultant and the treating mental health professionals will hold all information obtained from the patient in confidence. In the absence of a subpoena, the mental health professional is under no legal obligation to reveal any confidential information about the patient to outside parties, including the police. Any senior executive who is undergoing evaluation or treatment will be encouraged to sign a release-of-information statement allowing the mental health consultant and the treating mental health professionals to release information about the executive's condition to the senior corporate personnel officer. However, the impaired executive is under no obligation to sign the release-of-information statement.

Responsibilities of Key Parties

Impaired Senior Executive   All senior executives are encouraged to seek assistance by contacting their immediate superior and the senior personnel officer when they suspect that they are developing a problem with alcoholism, drug abuse, or mental illness that is impairing their job performance. If the senior personnel officer recommends an evaluation by the company's mental health consultant, who, after evaluation, subsequently recommends treatment, it is the responsibility of the executive in question to comply with the recommendation.

Immediate Superior of the Impaired Executive   All members of top management are expected to monitor the overall job performance and productivity of all senior executives who report to them. They are to be alert to developing signs and symptoms of executive alcoholism, drug abuse, or mental illness and the accompanying deterioration in job performance. The periodic monitoring for signs and symptoms of distress and deteriorating job performance is crucial to prompt detection and treatment of the impaired executive. If the immediate superior is concerned about a senior executive who is performing poorly and appears to be developing alcoholism, drug abuse, or mental illness, he or she should take the following specific steps.

First, collect as many data as possible from as many sources as possible that confirm that the troubled senior executive's job performance and overall occupational functioning have significantly declined. Document in writing the time, date, and nature of all instances of poor performance and all inappropriate, bizarre, out-of-character behaviors and their probable impact on the troubled senior executive's job performance. The time frame for collecting the data is different in each case; if the symptoms are serious, a good data collection effort should take no more than several days to several weeks.

Second, review and analyze all collected data in detail. Ask two questions: Is the troubled senior executive showing a significant decline in job performance? Is the executive's deteriorating job performance most likely a consequence of a problem with alcohol, drug abuse, or mental illness? If the answer to these questions is no, one need go no further. If the answer to both questions is yes, one can proceed with a plan of intervention. If, however, the senior executive appears to be performing in a competent to outstanding manner but still appears to be experiencing some "personal difficulties," do not intervene.

Third, arrange a meeting with the senior executive responsible for personnel matters to review all the data. Fourth, on the recommendation of the senior personnel officer, present the data on the impaired senior executive to the firm's mental health consultant. Fifth, if a formal evaluation by the company's mental health consultant is recommended, meet with the impaired senior executive and the senior personnel executive to review the data that support the findings of deteriorating job performance and psychological distress. Recommend that the impaired senior executive undergo a one-to-two-hour evaluation by the mental health consultant. Sixth, if after an evaluation by the mental health consultant the impaired executive is recommended for treatment, meet with the impaired executive, prior to the initiation of treatment, to discuss any concerns he or she may have.

Senior Corporate Personnel Officer   The role of the senior corporate personnel officer is to

- analyze all data presented to her or him for evidence of deteriorating job performance and developing signs and symptoms of alcoholism, drug abuse, or mental illness in a senior executive
- discuss all cases of possible senior executive impairment with the company's mental health consultant
- meet with the immediate superior and the impaired senior executive in question to recommend a formal evaluation by the mental health consultant
- meet with the impaired senior executive prior to treatment to answer any questions or address any concerns if treatment is recommended
- keep in close contact with the inpatient mental health treatment team and periodically visit the impaired senior executive during the inpatient treatment phase to discuss progress
- meet with the inpatient and aftercare treatment teams to plan and discuss aftercare treatment plans
- assist in reintegrating the recovering executive into the firm
- plan and assist in training of senior executives in the early

detection of executive alcoholism, drug abuse, and mental illness
- attend training for the improvement of her or his own knowledge about impaired executives
- assist in the ongoing evaluation of the impaired senior executive program

Mental Health Consultant   The primary function of the mental health consultant is to evaluate and assist the impaired executive in dealing promptly and effectively with a developing problem with alcoholism, drug abuse, or mental illness that is responsible for deteriorating job performance. This role includes

- conducting a formal evaluation of impaired senior executives; making an assessment of the need for treatment; and, if appropriate, convincing the impaired senior executives to accept treatment
- assisting the senior personnel officer in developing a list of treatment resources for impaired executives
- assisting in getting impaired executives into appropriate treatment facilities
- assisting the senior personnel representative in maintaining close contact with the inpatient mental health facility treatment professionals
- being involved in planning appropriate aftercare plans
- assisting the senior personnel officer in helping recovering executives reintegrate into the company
- conducting training of senior executives in the early detection of executive alcoholism, drug abuse, and mental illness
- assuring the confidentiality of records and information about impaired executives
- monitoring policies and procedures of the program to ensure that impaired executives' legal rights are not violated

Summary

There are a number of important components to a successful company policy on the detection and successful management of the alcoholic, drug-addicted, or mentally ill senior executive. These components include (1) statements about the policy's overall mission and justification and (2) a clear delineation of the roles and responsibilities of key parties, including the impaired senior executive, his or her immediate superior, the senior personnel officer, and the mental health consultant.

11

≈≈≈≈≈≈≈≈≈≈≈≈≈≈≈≈≈≈≈≈≈≈≈≈≈≈≈≈≈≈≈≈≈≈≈

Selecting a Mental Health
Consultant and Addressing
Other Issues

Choosing a Mental Health Consultant

The first and most important step is selecting a well-trained and experienced mental health consultant. The professional community of mental health professionals contains many individuals with a wide variety of experience and professional degrees. For example, a psychiatrist has graduated with an M.D. degree from a recognized school of medicine, has completed four or five years of postgraduate training as an intern and resident in psychiatry at a recognized medical center, is licensed by a state board of medical examiners in the state in which she or he practices, and, in many cases, has taken and passed a rigorous examination leading to certification in psychiatry offered by the American Board of Neurology and Psychiatry. A clinical psychologist has a master's, Ph.D., or equivalent degree and supervised postgraduate experience. To become licensed as a practicing psychologist, the individual must meet specific state licensing and certification requirements. A clinical nurse specialist has specialized in psychiatric nursing, holds a master's degree in the discipline, and is licensed by the state. A counselor usually has a master's or Ph.D. degree in a counseling discipline from an approved university. Due to the lack of consistent state licensing procedures, the background, training, and general qualifications of counselors can vary significantly. Although most counselors are very capable, competent, and experienced, it is important to fully investigate the credentials of any "counselor," including membership in nationally recognized professional associations. A psychiatric social worker has a master's degree from an accredited school of social work and is licensed to practice in the state of residence.

The mental health professional should have some experience in both inpatient and outpatient treatments and should also be experienced in alcohol and drug abuse. The mental health consultant should also be familiar with working with business organizations and their impaired executives. Probably the least effective way of finding a mental health consultant is by looking in the local telephone directory. The best and easiest way to find a competent local mental health consultant is to ask executives in other local firms for recommendations. Another good method is to call a department of psychiatry, social work, psychology, business administration, or counseling at the local university. The chairpersons of these departments are often quite happy to provide a list of suitable candidates. After obtaining a list of four or five candidates, write each of them a letter stating your interest in their services. In the letter state that you are interested in retaining their services on a part-time basis. In the letter also ask that they send a short statement of their training and experience, three professional references, an updated curriculum vitae, and their hourly rate for services.

After you receive the information from the candidates, arrange for them to be interviewed for approximately thirty minutes each by the senior executive responsible for all personnel and human resource matters in the firm. In reviewing credentials look for the quality of educational institutions attended, nature and duration of any advanced postdoctoral professional training, type and level of experience consulting to business organizations, quality of references, hourly fee, state licensing and certification, and membership in local and national professional bodies. Check references whenever possible to get a sense of the mental health professional's local reputation and the overall quality of his or her work. In the interview look for poise, ability to communicate in a direct and clear manner, and general interest and enthusiasm.

Once all candidates have been interviewed, review the data for each candidate and rank them according to your preference. A key element in the final selection is your perception of the mental health professional's ability to be available on short notice and her or his interest in working intensively over time with a variety of key players in the impaired senior executive's life, including the impaired executive's boss, the firm's senior executive in charge of personnel matters, the impaired executive's family, the professionals at the inpatient mental health facility, and the outpatient mental health treatment professionals.

Identification of Treatment Resources in the Community

In most instances, the treatment decision will be made by the mental health consultant in conjunction with the impaired senior executive after evaluation of the executive has been completed. Nevertheless, it is important that the senior personnel executive of the firm have a working knowledge of the treatment options available in the community so that he or she can provide appropriate input to the treatment decision. This is important for several reasons. First, not all treatment facilities and mental health professionals are created equal. Some have higher standards of care than others. Being an educated consumer who is involved with the treatment decision and able to distinguish among the different community treatment facilities and mental health professionals will increase the likelihood that the troubled senior executive will get timely, high-quality care. Second, treatment for alcoholism, drug abuse, or mental illness is costly and time-consuming. High prices and high quality do not necessarily go hand in hand. Showing an interest, being involved, and expressing concern about cost issues will ensure that the treating facility and the mental health professionals will pay attention to concerns about cost. Third, being involved ensures that the treatment facility will work cooperatively with the firm in coordinating all aspects of care and aftercare. Last of all, the plan for continuing and appropriate care as needed after discharge is a crucial component of any long-term treatment of a senior executive troubled by alcoholism, drug abuse, or mental illness. A working knowledge of the treatment options within the community will allow one to distinguish between those institutions and treatment providers who are willing, able, and motivated to work with the firm and the troubled senior executive on issues of continuing care after discharge and those facilities that show little desire to actively participate in appropriate aftercare planning.

There are many different types of inpatient mental health facilities, including county and state psychiatric hospitals, private for-profit and nonprofit psychiatric hospitals, psychiatric units in private and public voluntary general hospitals, and psychiatric units in Veterans Administration hospitals. Semiinstitutional mental health facilities include therapeutic communities, day hospitals, night hospitals, and halfway houses. These facilities differ in size, reputation, quality of medical staff, cost, treatment styles, and staffing resources. In these settings the troubled senior executive will receive a wide variety of treatments, depending on the diagnosis and individual treatment needs.

The semiinstitutional facilities, otherwise referred to as partial hospitalization (day hospitals, night hospitals, and halfway houses), are reserved for the individual who has received the maximum therapeutic benefit from an inpatient hospital stay but who still requires a level of intensity of services and treatments that cannot be provided in an outpatient setting. The treatment is usually during the day, the night, or on weekends. The programs provide many of the same types of services that are found in the inpatient setting, including the medical, psychiatric, and social interventions. The emphasis in the program is to assist the patient in developing the skills, resources, and psychological stability to move into an outpatient setting and return to full social and occupational functioning. A less intense transition step from the hospital to the outpatient setting is the community residence, whch includes the halfway house, the quarterway house, supervised cooperative apartments, and residential care facilities. Each facility has its own philosophy, approach, and goals, with some facilities specializing exclusively in the rehabilitation of alcoholics recently discharged from an in-patient facility. The therapeutic community is a specialized community residence for individuals with severe problems of chemical abuse and addiction. These nonprofessionally oriented self-help treatment centers focus on inducing significant change in the addict's character, personality, and behavior. Through abstinence, intense group encounters, reeducation, and physical work, these centers seek to turn drug addicts and abusers back into responsible citizens.

What does one need to know about the differences among the various inpatient and semiinstitutional mental health treatment facilities available to treat the troubled senior executive? First, one must have a working knowledge of the types of problems and patients that a given mental health facility has the most success in treating. Some institutions are good with adolescents. Others specialize in geriatric patients. Others cater exclusively to alcoholics and drug abusers. Still others focus on long-term psychiatric hospitalization of the severely chronically mentally ill. Very few institutions do an outstanding job across the board. Ask the mental health consultant. Consult with executive colleagues at other firms. Find out where senior executives and their dependents are getting treatment in the community. Visit a few facilities and ask the staffs for their opinion of what patients or problems they work well with. Finally, pick the facility that seems to do the best job for the specific problem that the executive is experiencing.

Second, be aware that most private mental health facilities receive the bulk of their revenues from reimbursements from third-party private insurance carriers. Because of the level of reimbursement, these private institutions can usually afford to devote more resources to the treatment of their patients than can public institutions that are funded through government revenues. Greater resources translates into greater staff-to-patient ratios and more intense and daily treatment rendered, resulting in some cases in more rapid and complete recovery of the troubled executive. Also, as a general rule, greater resources usually attract higher-caliber mental health professionals, both as attending and as full-time and part-time staff members, although there are exceptions in every community. There are a number of very excellent public mental treatment facilities around the country, but due to funding difficulties and the escalating cost of inpatient mental health care, their numbers have dwindled significantly over the last thirty years. Find out through colleagues, friends, and mental health professionals in the community which mental health facilities have the greatest resources available for the treatment of alcoholism, drug abuse, and mental illness.

Third, be aware which mental health facilities have the shortest stays with the best outcomes for alcoholism, drug abuse, and mental illness. This information can usually be obtained from the admissions office of the mental health treatment facility. Length of stay is expressed in average number of days of hospitalization per admission. One gross measure of outcomes is percentage of annual admissions that are readmissions rather than first admissions. Getting a troubled senior executive back to normal is important to both the executive and the firm, which needs the executive to return as quickly as possible to his or her job responsibilities. Although longer stays are more expensive than shorter stays, longer stays do not necessarily translate into better or more effective treatment.

Last of all, check the mental health facility's track record in assisting patients in making adequate continuing care plans after being discharged. Many mental health facilities have their own aftercare programs tailored to the needs of their patients, but some do not. The success of the troubled senior executive's reintegration into the firm and the community will greatly depend on the executive's having a solid and appropriate continuing care plan after discharge. Ask the admissions office who handles the aftercare planning, when the aftercare planning begins (optimally, the day the executive arrives at the facility), and if the professionals in charge of aftercare plans will be willing to work closely with the firm in designing an optimal plan.

Many outpatient mental health therapies are available, including several hundred different schools of psychotherapeutic thought with their own philosophies and treatment techniques. Many outpatient psychotherapies have their origin in Freud's theories about the workings of the human psyche. The basic premise underlying all psychotherapy is that by engaging in a relationship with the psychotherapist, the individual enhances his or her ability to decrease emotional distress and to increase social and occupational functioning. The outpatient therapies generally fall into two major categories: the insight-oriented psychotherapies and the behavioral therapies. The behavioral therapists emphasize concrete and specific techniques to bring about change in certain types of maladaptive behaviors while deemphasizing underlying causes and childhood antecedents to the given behavior. The insight-oriented psychotherapists explore the psychological or unconscious underpinnings of the patient's behavior and through this insight bring about behavioral change.

What does one need to know about the outpatient options available to the recovering senior executive? First, pay attention to the cost, both per session and projected total for the treatment. Therapies differ both in the dollars per session and in the total cost, depending on the length of time the recovering senior executive will be in treatment. Costs differ also with regard to demand; geographic locale; therapist's professional background, training, and experience; and prior arrangements with participating firms, that is, preferred provider contracts. As with inpatient treatment, high cost does not necessarily correlate with high quality. Review the firm's insurance coverage with regard to exclusions, copayments, annual sessions per year and total dollar caps, and deductibles. Question the proposed outpatient psychotherapy professionals directly about dollar-per-session costs, whether those costs are expected to go up over the course of the treatment, what the total costs of the treatment are expected to be, competitors' costs for similar treatments, and whether they accept reimbursement from the firm's insurance carrier.

Second, one should make sure that the proposed outpatient treatment professionals are well trained, experienced, and respected in the local professional community. Ask them about universities they graduated from and where they received their postgraduate training. Find out whether they are experi-

enced with the particular disorder of the recovering senior executive and with recovering senior executives in general. Determine
whether they are willing to work closely with other concerned
members of the community who are assisting the executive in
his or her recovery, whether concerned colleagues from the
executive's firm, supportive family members, friends, probation
officers, or sponsors from Alcoholics Anonymous, Narcotics
Anonymous, or Emotions Anonymous.

Third, inquire about whether the proposed treating professionals have the interest, time, and motivation to be in communication with the firm's designated executive who will be
monitoring the recovering executive's progress. It is important
that the recovering senior executive sign a release-of-information
statement so that information can flow between the treating
professionals and the firm's designated executive. The designated executive needs to know on an ongoing basis how the
treatment is going, how the executive is progressing, whether
the executive is showing up for treatment sessions, and whether
the executive is paying his or her bills. In addition, the designated officer will have a need to report to the treating professional unusual, unexpected, or concerning behavior on the part
of the recovering senior executive in order to receive guidance
about what, if any, action to take. The designated executive will
need to seek advice from the treating professional about significant changes in the senior executive's job responsibilities, including pending transfers, proposed promotions or demotion,
and possible changes in overall job responsibilities.

Education and Training of Executives

The next important step in an organizational strategy is to educate and train the senior executive ranks in the detection and
management of executive mental illness. These training sessions
will be run by the senior personnel executive, his representatives, and the mental health consultant. The sessions should begin with a large-group format and then break into small groups
to go over prepared cases that the senior executives attempt to

deal with. All senior executives should be trained in the detection of symptoms and signs, work performance documentation, and when to talk to personnel representatives. There should be opportunity for role playing with the senior executives who are training to present their data to the senior personnel executive for review. There should be a mix of cases, and each participant should do a number of different cases. All new senior executives should be required to undergo this training, and all executives in the organization should undergo this training and should update their skills around these procedures once every two years. In addition to formal training, the senior executive ranks should be kept up to date about alcohol, drug abuse, and treatment and rehabilitation issues with general lectures and presentations by experts. These sessions should be mandatory and should occur several times a year. It is important to also educate the families of senior executives through voluntary evening meetings about executive drug abuse, alcoholism, and mental illness.

Review of Current Company Sick-Leave Policies, Mental Health Insurance Coverage, and Temporary and Permanent Medical Disability Insurance Coverage

A stay at an inpatient mental health treatment facility is expensive. The total cost of a twenty-eight-day inpatient stay in a private psychiatric facility can range anywhere from $7,000 to more than $25,000. Differences in daily hospital rates are, in part, a reflection of demand, overhead costs, profit, required return on capital, reputation, style of treatment, and regional custom. Given the expense of inpatient mental health treatment, it is important to be knowledgeable about prices as expressed in dollars per day. Although private mental health facilities can, on the average, devote more resources to the treatment of their patients than public institutions, they are also considerably more expensive. Beware of costs not included in the daily rate, including laboratory tests, general medical or neurological consultations, psychiatric attending visit fees, psychological tests, and various daily or weekly patient therapies. Ask the admissions office for a detailed list of all the extra charges likely to be incurred during the course of the treatment and request the figures for the average total cost for a typical inpatient stay for alcoholism, drug abuse, or mental illness. Shop around for the best price consistent with a high quality of care. For example, some psychiatric units in private voluntary hospitals in the community may offer comparable quality inpatient care with a shorter average length of stay at lower daily cost than the local for-profit private psychiatric hospital. Also, many executives may feel less stigmatized in a psychiatric bed in a general hospital than in a completely psychiatric facility. Many mental health institutions, through preferred provider and other financial arrangements, may offer substantial discounts off the posted daily rate. Whenever possible and prudent, use outpatient treatment facilities. For example, outpatient alcohol detoxification can be quite effective, particularly with individuals who are cooperative and have strong support from their families. Inpatient detoxification, although considerably more expensive, is usually required for alcoholics who are at risk for delirium tremens, severely depressed or suicidal, confused and unable to comprehend their situation, psychotic, or just generally uncooperative, unreliable, or unable to remain sober on their own through the detoxification process.

Most treatment obtained at an inpatient mental health facility will be covered by the senior executive's private group health insurance policy offered through the firm. Private policies are offered by private insurance carriers, Blue Cross and Blue Shield, and group practice plans, including health maintenance organizations (HMOs), preferred provider organizations (PPOs), independent practice associations (IPAs), and so on. Increasingly, major corporations in this country are financing their employee health care on a self-insurance basis as a way to contain costs and control utilization. The typical group health insurance policy will reimburse the executive for 80 percent of inpatient or outpatient charges, although coverage for inpatient and outpatient care can vary significantly with the plan and the insurance carrier. Usually the coverage for inpatient mental health treatment is more generous than the coverage for outpatient psychiatric care. Many private insurance plans contain deductibles, copayments, and a limit on the number of inpatient hospitalizations, outpatient psychotherapy sessions, or inpatient stays per calendar year.

In addition, insurance carriers commonly put caps on the lifetime benefits for mental health services, typically at $50,000. Many employers and their insurance carriers have entered into agreements with a variety of health care providers to provide services cheaply or at a discount. HMOs, PPOs, and IPAs have been the main beneficiaries of these new arrangements. HMOs provide complete medical care on a prepaid basis. In general, the length of inpatient stays for patients enrolled in an HMO is significantly shorter than for patients enrolled in other private insurance plans. These new providers use a variety of techniques to effectively limit their mental health care costs, including pre-screening programs to determine if hospitalization is warranted, mandatory second opinions, precertification for major procedures, concurrent review, retrospective review, and strict utilization review of services. Before recommending a specific mental health treatment facility to a troubled senior executive, check that the firm's insurance plan is adequate to cover the projected total cost. If the insurance plan does not provide adequate coverage for alcoholism, drug abuse, or mental illness, it is important to get an appropriate plan in place quickly. At today's costs for mental health care, no firm and no senior executive, no matter how financially sound, can shoulder the burden for a prolonged period of time.

The fourth step is review of health insurance, disability insurance, medical retirement, and sick-leave policy. There are many different types of health insurance carrier. The one the current firm has may be adequate for physical illnesses, but do not assume that it will be adequate for mental illnesses. Be sure to read the fine print about coverage for mental illness. Be sure to notice the issue of copayments, deductibles, yearly limitations on admissions, yearly dollar limitations, and lifetime dollar caps. Also look carefully at the issue of treatment for drug and alcohol abuse. Be prepared to change carriers to get one with a better policy with regard to coverage of mental health treatment. Reviewing the policies is very important to the financing of mental health coverage. The cost of inpatient mental health treatment can run in excess of $500 a day.

Ongoing Evaluation and Review
of Impaired Executive Program

The last issue is evaluation and review of the entire impaired senior executive program. It is necessary to know over time if the time and effort to deal with the impaired employee are worthwhile. Keep the evaluation simple and cost-effective. The best way to do this is to plan for it when the entire program is planned, but also keep in mind that any good evaluation process evolves over time. A periodic comprehensive review of the status of the program will involve an assessment from everyone involved in the program, including the senior executives who have been through the program and are recovering or are recovered from alcoholism, drug abuse, or mental illness, and their families; the designated senior personnel executive in charge of the program; the mental health consultant; and the mental health treatment providers. Although evaluation of the program is in itself costly and time-consuming, the purpose of evaluation is to get a better program at lower cost that detects, treats, and returns to work all impaired senior executives.

There are two major program components to evaluate: the process of dealing with the impaired senior executive and the outcome of the program. In terms of the process of dealing with the impaired executive, the specific issues are access to the program, utilization of the program, effectiveness of the referral, maintenance of confidentiality, and cost of the treatment. In terms of the outcome, the important information is whether the impaired senior executives who went through the program actually got better and improved their performance. Let us review each component separately and in more detail.

First is the issue of access. Look at the sources of the referrals—how many were self-referred and how many were referred by other senior executives; there should be a balance. Second is the issue of utilization of the program. It is important to know what the major performance deficits were: for example, absenteeism and lateness, missing deadlines, or interpersonal disruption. You should know the basic demographics of the senior executives, including age, sex, race, title, and location in the firm; you should also know about the distinction between mental illness and drug and alcohol problems.

Third, learn which mental health treatment referrals were successful and which were not. This information is needed to continue dealing with those mental health care providers who are successful and cooperate and to avoid dealing with those who are not. Fourth, learn about the treatment. What type of treatment did the senior executive receive, how long did the treatment take, how much inpatient and how much outpatient treatment did he or she receive, and what was the total cost of the treatment? With this type of information it is possible to negotiate with mental health treatment providers to get higher-quality care, in the shortest time possible, at the lowest possible cost.

In terms of outcome, there are a number of pieces of information that are needed and useful. It is important to know if the senior executives returned to work full time or part time and how long it took for the recovering executive to get back to full performance. It is also important to know what percentage of treated executives were not able to come back to the work force and had to be placed on permanent medical disability. This information is useful in determining how expensive the impaired senior executive is to the company and how to deal with this cost.

Summary

There are a number of steps to be taken in developing and implementing a successful organizational strategy for the detection and successful management of the alcoholic, drug-addicted, or mentally ill senior executive. These steps include (1) selecting a mental health consultant; (2) identifying specific community treatment resources; (3) training company senior executives; (4) reviewing sick-leave policies, disability insurance, and group health insurance; and (5) developing an evaluation procedure.

12

~~~~~~

Responding to the Challenge
of the Impaired Executive:
Case Studies

The previous chapters have covered a variety of topics, including case studies of impaired executives, suggestions for getting and keeping the impaired executive in treatment, managing the recovering executive's return to work, and organizational strategies for effectively dealing with the impaired executive. It will be appropriate now to give case examples of how several organizations and their mental health consultants successfully met the challenge of dealing with the impaired senior executive. Although the cases are real, both the individuals and the circumstances of the cases have been heavily disguised to maintain confidentiality.

Case of the Disturbed Executive

I was retained as a mental health consultant to the newly organized employee-assistance program that was put into place for hourly employees and supervisory managers of a large East Coast manufacturing firm. When the program was conceptualized, the firm's senior vice-president for human resources had rejected my suggestion that a separate program be initiated for impaired senior managers. He cited "little need" for such an effort. One afternoon, while I was on site consulting with a member of the firm's EAP staff about a troubled hourly employee, I received a frantic call from the human resources vice-president, who stated that Ms. C, the senior vice-president for marketing, was "lying on the floor of her office in a very agitated state and refusing to speak to anyone." I rushed over to the office of Ms. C, who was, indeed, lying on the floor in the fetal position, rocking back and forth, and refusing to speak, while several of the office staff and the senior vice-president for human resources were kneeling by her side. I asked to be left alone with Ms. C for a few minutes. I managed to coax out of her that she had been seeing a psychiatrist, whose name and telephone number she volunteered, along with permission to contact him. I got in touch with the psychiatrist, who indicated that during the last several months Ms. C had been suffering from moderate depression and was being considered for medication. The psychiatrist quickly agreed with my suggestion that we admit Ms. C immediately to a local mental health facility for observation; she consented and was admitted that afternoon.

When I discussed the incident the next day with the senior vice-president for human resources, he admitted that several days prior Ms. C had mentioned in passing that she was "feeling tense" and felt that her work was suffering. At that point the senior vice-president for human resources suggested that Ms. C seek help at the EAP, but Ms. C never followed up on this suggestion. Recognizing that Ms. C was a highly valued and indispensable member of the senior management team who had never before experienced difficulties of any kind, the senior vice-president for human resources asked me to become involved with the case to monitor Ms. C's treatment and to assist with a plan for reintegrating her into the firm. I agreed. I met with Ms. C in the hospital and received her permission to be in contact with her inpatient treatment team, her outpatient psychiatrist, and the senior vice-president for human resources about Ms. C's treatment and future.

After discussions with key individuals, I discovered that Ms. C was fifty years old and had become severely depressed after her husband died from cancer six months earlier. Her job performance gradually deteriorated as she became increasingly depressed and upset. Because she had a reputation as a "loner" at the firm, she did not reach out to others for support. Although she was aware of the services of the firm's EAP, she felt uncomfortable seeking help from a program that was set up for hourly employees. She was also concerned about the issue of confidentiality. I reported to the senior vice-president for human resources that Ms. C's inpatient treatment team had indicated that she was being stabilized on an antidepressant, was making good progress, and was scheduled to be discharged within two and one-half weeks. During the last week of Ms. C's stay, the senior vice-president for human resources, myself, the outpatient psychiatrist, Ms. C, and the inpatient treatment team convened a meeting to discuss aftercare treatment. We decided that Ms. C would return to work, continue her medication, and continue her outpatient therapy. She returned to work and showed a significant improvement in her job performance and overall demeanor. She was less depressed, became more outgoing, and reached out for support from her colleagues.

Several weeks later I again approached the senior vice-president for human resources about instituting a formal company policy and program for impaired senior executives. Although he still did not see the need for a formal policy or program, he consented to several training sessions for the senior executive ranks on the management of the impaired senior executive.

There are a number of things that this case points up about organizational management of the impaired senior executive. First, although employee-assistance programs serve a very important function in an organization, this case illustrates that such programs can be underutilized by senior management. A formal corporate program for the impaired senior executive in this firm might have convinced Ms. C to seek help sooner. Second, this case illustrates that a senior executive can experience a crisis quite suddenly and unexpectedly. Having a formal corporate policy in place and a set of procedures to follow in the management of the impaired senior executive would allow the organization to act quickly and effectively. Third, the senior vice-president for human resources, had he been more aware of the signs and symptoms of mental distress because of a corporate training program, might have sought assistance for Ms. C earlier in the course of her illness. Fourth, good communication among the recovering senior executive, the mental health consultant, the treating professionals, and the senior vice-president for human resources is crucial to the eventual success of reintegrating the recovering senior executive into the firm. Fifth, although the senior vice-president for human resources consented to training for the senior executive ranks, training without a formal corporate policy and set of procedures is not enough. Senior executives must be trained, but they also must know how to act in the context of a formal corporate policy and program for the impaired senior executive.

Case of the "Psychotic" Executive

Dr. Jay B. Rohrlich is a board-certified psychiatrist and mental health consultant who works extensively with impaired executives and whose office is located in New York City. Dr. Rohrlich was called by the chairman and CEO of a large computer firm. Although the firm had no formal corporate policy on the impaired senior executive, the chairman took a personal interest in the health and welfare of all the members of his senior executive team.

The chairman had called to discuss the chief financial officer, Mr. D, who was frightening the other executives and employees with his behavior. The chairman had noted that Mr. D was working increasingly long hours alone in his office. The chairman had personally observed that Mr. D would often slam phones, gesture wildly to no one in particular, yell in frustration, and sometimes pull his hair out. This behavior had become evident within the last several months and was out of character for Mr. D, who was generally known to be a shy and retiring person. The chairman related that other executives and employees had complained to him that they were becoming afraid to talk with Mr. D or even to walk near the man's office. The chairman was informed by another senior executive that Mr. D was observed talking and gesturing to pigeons on the sidewalk outside the building where the firm's corporate headquarters were located. Yet, in spite of his increasingly disturbing behavior, Mr. D, as reported by the chairman, was a loyal, highly competent, and quite indispensable senior executive who had an extraordinary mastery of highly complex and technical financial matters. The quality of his work continued to be very high. Although the chairman had not talked directly to Mr. D or shared his concerns with the firm's senior personnel officer, the chairman knew that something had to be done. He was calling Dr. Rohrlich for advice because he did not want to jump to ill-conceived conclusions or to act with an insufficient understanding of what Mr. D might be experiencing. Dr. Rohrlich agreed that Mr. D appeared to be in distress and recommended that the chairman confront Mr. D with what he was doing and refer him for a psychiatric evaluation. The chairman, hoping that Mr. D's symptoms would abate without intervention and realizing that since Mr. D's job performance had not deteriorated he could not be forced to be evaluated or treated, decided to "leave well enough alone." A year and a half later the chairman called Dr. Rohrlich to refer Mr. D for an evaluation. The chairman reported that Mr. D's behavior had worsened after some quieting the year before. His work performance had also deteriorated. The chairman had confronted Mr. D about his deteriorating job performance and inappropriate behavior and strongly suggested that Mr. D undergo a psychological evaluation, to which he agreed.

Dr. Rohrlich saw Mr. D in his office. On evaluation, Mr. D turned out to be a very shy fifty-four-year-old who kept to himself both professionally and personally. He had never married and was constantly being called at the office by his hysterical widowed mother, which caused him great frustration and led to his slamming the phone. He was, in reality, a nonpsychotic very socially inhibited man, extremely shy and wishing others would befriend him. In his loneliness he sometimes talked to animals. Mr. D signed a release-of-information statement that allowed Dr. Rohrlich to call the chairman to report that Mr. D was not psychotic, not dangerous, and that people in the firm should reach out to him more and make him feel more comfortable. Dr. Rohrlich also recommended to Mr. D that he meet weekly with Dr. Rohrlich to learn how to be more aware of his

impact on others and how to control and channel his frustra-
tions more appropriately while continuing at his job. Inpatient
hospitalization was judged to be neither desirable nor necessary.
Mr. D agreed to see Dr. Rohrlich regularly. Within a short time,
Mr. D was able to control his behavior at work and to improve
his job performance. This improvement in his behavior led to a
much more amiable relationship between him and his fellow
executives. He became more outgoing with them, and their fears
abated as well.

This case illustrates a number of important points about
the management of the troubled senior executive. First, not all
senior executives who appear to be "seriously disturbed" are, in
fact, alcoholic, drug-abusing, or seriously mentally ill. Second,
although the chairman did not have a formal corporate policy
on the impaired executive, he was able to monitor the behavior
of his senior executive team due to his personal interest in their
health and welfare. In this case, institution of a formal policy
on the impaired senior executive might have allowed the chairman to delegate the responsibility of dealing with Mr. D to his
senior corporate personnel officer, who might have had more
experience or, at least, added an additional perspective. In addition, formal training of this firm's senior executive team in the
management of the impaired senior executive might have per-
mitted others at the senior level to appropriately intervene early
on. Mr. D may have even voluntarily sought assistance earlier if
he had been aware of the signs and symptoms of psychological
distress.

The third important point is that the chairman was careful and was willing to wait for up to a year and one-half, until it
was clear that Mr. D's unusual behavior was adversely affecting
his job performance. This gave the chairman the leverage to convince Mr. D to be evaluated and eventually treated while at the
same time protecting the chairman and the firm against accusations of harassment or discrimination. The fourth point is that
the chairman had immediate access to a qualified mental health
consultant who was experienced in dealing with executive impairment. This access allowed for a first-rate evaluation and subsequent effective treatment. The fifth and last point is that

there was good communication between the chairman, Mr. D, and the mental health consultant that allowed an appropriate management of this troubling case.

Case of the Harasser

Dr. Peter Brill is a board-certified psychiatrist, founder and president of Integra, Inc., located in Philadelphia, Pennsylvania, and consultant to a variety of corporations. Dr. Brill was called by the president of a large defense-related company about the company's vice-president and director of government relations, Mr. E. Female employees in the firm had been calling the president during the past year complaining that Mr. E was sexually harassing them. At first, the president did not act on the complaints, believing that it was all "a tempest in a teapot." He considered Mr. E to be a highly valued senior executive who had been instrumental in getting several large defense contracts and who continued to perform in a highly competent manner. Within the company, Mr. E, who held a Ph.D. degree, was considered a brilliant engineer, but he was also a highly volatile personality who, without warning, would rant and rage at executives and office staff alike. There was no corporate policy that formally addressed the issue of troubled or troubling senior executives—the president preferred to handle these matters himself on a case-by-case basis. In the last several months, however, the president had noted that Mr. E's performance had slipped somewhat. Only after a female employee who had been sexually harassed by him had called the president and threatened to contact a lawyer did the president decide to call Dr. Brill for advice on how to cope with Mr. E. Dr. Brill suggested that the president confront Mr. E about his deteriorating job performance and inappropriate behavior and recommend an evaluation by Dr. Brill. Mr. E, when confronted by the president, denied that his job performance had slipped, defended his behavior toward the female employees as being "harmless," and refused to see a "shrink" because he was not "crazy." Only after the president raised the possibility of disciplinary action did Mr. E reluctantly agree to see Dr. Brill.

Dr. Brill met with Mr. E. He was a forty-five-year-old, red-faced, slightly overweight, rapidly talking, charming individual who basically took the attitude that this was much ado about nothing. Dr. Brill told Mr. E that he was evaluating Mr. E for the company and requested that Mr. E sign a release-of-information statement, which he did. Mr. E had married three years earlier for the third time. He felt that his wife did not understand him. They were also having sexual problems. He complained that she would often become "irrationally" angry at him and refuse to talk to him for days. He denied any problems with drugs or alcohol. Dr. Brill asked if he could meet with Mr. E's wife alone, and after some reluctance Mr. E agreed. The wife reported a completely different story. She said that her husband was a heavy drinker. He would frequently gulp down five or six cocktails before dinner, followed by a bottle or two of wine with his meal. During weekends he would consume "a couple of fifths" and "black out." Dr. Brill also learned from the wife that Mr. E had one driving-while-intoxicated charge that was still pending, would often become verbally abusive with her when he was intoxicated, and recently had begun drinking in the morning before he went to work to "calm his morning shakes." Dr. Brill then met again with Mr. E and confronted him about his drinking. He at first adamantly denied that his drinking was out of control and that he was an alcoholic, but he did admit to a steady increase in his drinking during the past three years, which was of some concern to him. Dr. Brill recommended to Mr. E that he enter a thirty-day alcohol-rehabilitation program. Mr. E refused. Dr. Brill then called the president of the firm and told him that Mr. E had a significant problem with alcohol that needed immediate attention. The president met with Mr. E the next day and, with the threat of disciplinary action, persuaded him to seek treatment. Mr. E entered an alcohol-rehabilitation program and did well; he returned to work immediately after his discharge. A back-to-work conference was arranged with the president, Mr. E, the senior corporate personnel officer, and Dr. Brill. A reduction of duties was structured for three months to allow Mr. E to attend daily Alcoholics Anonymous meetings and biweekly individual alcohol counseling.

Eventually, Mr. E returned to full work activities. Three years after the initial intervention, his marriage was doing well, and he remained sober. The president of the firm continued to handle all problems with his senior executives on a case-by-case basis without a formal corporate policy or set of procedures.

There are a number of things that this case points up about the organizational approach to the management of the impaired senior executive. First, "tempests in teapots" can often turn out to be much more than that when it comes to troubling behavior on the part of a senior executive. Perhaps the president would have intervened sooner if he had become more familiar with the signs and symptoms of executive alcoholism, drug abuse, and mental illness through a formal corporate training program. Second, had Mr. D also been educated about the early signs of alcoholism, he might have sought assistance earlier for his problem. Third, the presence of a formal corporate policy and the following of an established set of procedures on the management of the impaired senior executive might have protected both the president and the firm against any future filing of a work-related harassment or discrimination lawsuit by Mr. E. Fourth, another opinion and perspective, as could have been provided by the firm's senior personnel officer, might have allowed the president to act sooner. A formal corporate policy clearly stipulates who should be involved and when in dealing with the impaired senior executive. Fifth, the president was fortunate that he knew Dr. Brill, who happened to be available at the time. What would have happened if the president had not known of a capable mental health consultant or if Dr. Brill had not been available? A corporate policy on the impaired senior executive requires that a designated and available mental health consultant be an integral part of the present and future management of the impaired senior executive.

Summary

The above examples illustrate a number of advantages of a formal corporate policy and set of procedures for dealing with the impaired senior executive. First, impaired senior executives often have a strong resistance to availing themselves of the services of the firm's employee-assistance program that was designed for assisting hourly employees, supervisory managers, and middle managers. Second, a formal corporate policy and a clear set of procedures allow an organization to respond appropriately, quickly, and effectively to the distress of an impaired senior executive. Third, a formal program with a training and educational component will often allow for earlier intervention in the detection and management of the impaired senior executive. Fourth, a corporate program for the impaired senior executive will ensure that all appropriate members of the senior management team are involved in managing the impaired executive and that good communication occurs among all involved parties. A clear set of corporate procedures on managing the impaired senior executive, faithfully followed, is the best protection against accusations of harassment or discrimination by aggrieved senior executives.

13

~~~~~~

Conclusion:
Putting the Impaired
Executive in Perspective

Management Challenge of the Impaired Executive

The major challenge of top management and the key idea
on which this book rests is that the impaired senior executive
must be detected early, treated effectively, and reintegrated into
the firm. In this book I have introduced the reader to five senior
executives in crisis—Al; Victor, Jr.; Charlie; Jerry; and Ralph. I
have discussed the various and complex causes of alcoholism,
drug abuse, and mental illness; described the treatments that are
available for these disorders; and outlined the strategies for
early detection, treatment, and reintegration of the senior executive impaired by these disorders. I have challenged a popular
view that senior executives do not develop serious mental illness
and that they are all rational, stable individuals who always
manage according to reasonable organizational objectives. I have
maintained that top management can no longer afford to ignore
the possibility of alcoholism, drug abuse, and mental illness
within their senior executive ranks. I have explained how the
risk factors for the development of senior executive distress are
numerous, difficult to identify, and still harder to combat. I
have attempted to show that the alcoholic, drug-abusing, or
mentally ill senior executive, in a position of influence and responsibility, can profoundly influence and distort organizational

143

decision making, leadership, strategy, structure, and group functioning.

The cases of the five senior executives well illustrate how
alcoholism, illicit drug use, depression, bipolar illness, and
schizophrenia each can have a dramatic impact on the performance of the affected senior executive. If undiagnosed and untreated, these illnesses can quickly lead to poor decision making, lowered morale, and inadequate and ineffective leadership.
Alcoholic and drug-dependent senior executives will exhibit
poor business judgment, depressed senior executives will withdraw and neglect their responsibilities, manic senior executives
will behave impulsively without adequate forethought, and
paranoid senior executives will blame others and increase interpersonal conflict. Strategies that only partially address the problems of senior executive distress, including occasional executive
stress-management seminars, are unlikely to be very helpful.
These hit-or-miss programs usually focus on a few executive
symptoms without getting to root causes. They do not address
all the risk factors to which senior executives are exposed, nor
do they offer a comprehensive strategy for dealing with senior
executives in crisis. Without a sound knowledge of the root factors and causes, no solution for a senior executive's impairment
will be possible. Only the surface symptoms will be dealt with,
while the underlying problems and issues will remain untouched.
Dealing with an alcoholic, drug-dependent, or mentally ill senior
executive requires a comprehensive strategy that will convince
the executive that he or she has a major problem, show the
cause of the problem, and give a concrete plan of action to adequately deal with it.

Drawbacks and Limitations

I believe that a comprehensive program for the early detection,
treatment, and reintegration of the impaired senior executive
can more appropriately and effectively focus on all senior executives at risk of developing alcoholism, drug abuse, or mental
illness. Nevertheless, there are a number of drawbacks and limitations. The first drawback is that such a program is time-con-

suming and not easy to put in place. Top management must spend the time, energy, and resources to accomplish such a task. Significant amounts of time must be spent with senior executives overcoming their resistance to such a program and gaining their support. Just the thought of such a program will have a disquieting effect on those senior executives who may fear that it is a "cover" for an effort by top management to "thin" the senior executive ranks by labeling individuals psychologically "unfit."

The second drawback is the temptation to cut costs and save time by cutting the mental health consultant "out of the loop." It must be emphasized that a crucial determinant of the success of this approach is the involvement of the mental health consultant in all phases of the management of the impaired senior executive; eliminating the mental health consultant is ill advised. If the program is conducted entirely by the president of the firm, for example, without adequate professional input, there is the risk of significantly increasing the legal liability of the firm and the president and of doing more harm than good in the long run.

A third drawback is that this approach cannot guarantee that all impaired senior executives will be successfully rehabilitated and reintegrated into the firm. Some late-stage alcoholic, drug-dependent, or mentally ill senior executives will not be able to continue working. Most of the cases presented here have favorable outcomes, but I have also had failures. Some psychiatric problems are so severe and long-standing that they are not correctable even with the best treatment available. In addition, particularly with alcoholic and drug-dependent executives, impenetrable denial and lack of motivation may doom efforts at rehabilitation. Given these drawbacks and limitations, I offer my approach, not as the only answer but as one possible answer to a very difficult problem. Being successful with the impaired senior executive will require a long, time-consuming, and difficult intervention process. Although one may lose as many cases as one may win, the effort is surely worth making.

Resource

~~~~~~

A Primer on Psychotherapies
and Psychiatric Medications
for Impaired Executives

A number of psychotherapies and psychiatric medications are available for executives and other individuals impaired by alcoholism, drug abuse, or mental illness. Although these therapeutic interventions are no different for anyone, executive or not, who has become emotionally impaired, it is important for all executives to have at least a basic understanding of them.

Individual and Group Insight-Oriented Psychotherapy

Individual and group insight-oriented psychotherapies are inpatient or outpatient treatments conducted by an experienced mental health professional. The sessions vary in length from thirty minutes to an hour and one-half and in frequency from several times a week to once a month; they last for months to years depending on the problems treated. The individual insight-oriented psychotherapy treatment is one of the more expensive outpatient treatments, both in terms of dollars per session and in terms of total cost, while group insight-oriented psychotheraapy is less expensive. The treatments are usually covered by most employers' insurance plans but are frequently restricted by thirty-to-fifty-a-year session caps or a specific lifetime dollar cap.

Insight-oriented group psychotherapy is an inpatient or

outpatient psychotherapy conducted with a group of patients. In individual insight-oriented psychotherapy there are only the patient and the therapist. The goals of both therapies are to have the patient(s) identify the problems, understand the underlying psychological forces, and learn new ways of behaving to increase social and occupational functioning, all of which may take from several months to several years. In addition, the group members enhance the process of change because of the increased opportunity for interaction, discussion, feedback, and support. Optimal group size is usually between six and ten, with one or two group psychotherapists leading the group.

The recovering executive may find insight-oriented individual or group psychotherapy to be quite an adjustment. High-level, successful executives have a strong bias for action. They do not dwell on their innermost motives. Talking about feelings and other intimate details of one's life to total strangers is usually not part of an executive's past experience or mental set. In the beginning of treatment many executives may become frustrated because of the relative lack of feedback and the slow pace of progress and change. But if the executive perseveres, the treatment will usually turn out to be very helpful. Insight-oriented individual and group psychotherapists differ considerably in their experience in working with executives and in their desire to be in regular communication with the recovering executive's firm. One should inquire in advance.

What about the issue of insight-oriented individual or group psychotherapy for an executive who is primarily recovering from alcohol or drug abuse? After discharge recovering alcoholics or drug abusers may be required to attend up to ninety Alcoholics Anonymous or Narcotics Anonymous meetings in ninety days, in addition to other outpatient chemical-dependency treatment activities. After the alcoholic or chemical-dependent executive has been sober for three to six months, insight-oriented individual or group psychotherapy can become an option for those who have the interest, motivation, and problems best addressed by this form of treatment. But it is important to emphasize that, in and of themselves, the insight-oriented psychotherapies and the psychotherapies mentioned below are not designed for or capable of preventing the recovering executive from drinking or taking drugs.

Brief Therapy, Cognitive Therapy, and Behavioral Therapy

Brief therapy, cognitive therapy, and behavioral therapy are, in general, shorter-term psychotherapies that focus on a specific problem or concern. In brief therapy there are a rapid identification and understanding of the problem and the development of a specific strategy to deal with it. Cognitive therapy is a type of short-term therapy used primarily for anxiety and depression. The basic concept underlying the treatment is that self-defeating thoughts will lead to dysphoric mood states. The goal of the treatment is to correct dysfunctional thought patterns by having patients adopt more positive thoughts about the world and themselves. A course of treatment usually lasts ten to fifteen sessions.

Behavioral therapy, also known as behavior modification, is used in the treatment of specific problem behaviors, including phobias, weight problems and eating habits, smoking, compulsions, anxieties, and speech problems. The treatment focuses on observable events, particularly the behavior of the patient. The treatment uses a variety of behavioral techniques based on learning theories to modify behavior. The steps in the treatment include an analysis of reinforcing factors or disturbing situations that maintain behavior and the introduction of a set of exercises for decreasing, eliminating, or replacing undesirable behaviors with more adaptive ones. The techniques used include systematic desensitization, flooding, graded exposure, graded participant modeling, positive reinforcement, extinction, and negative reinforcement.

None of these three treatments deals with the patient's feelings toward the therapist or with the patient's deep-seated character problems or neurotic conflicts. The orientation of these therapies may be most in tune with the recovering executive's natural inclination toward short-term horizons, action, and an outcome. The other advantage of these therapies as compared to the longer-term insight-oriented psychotherapies is their relatively modest total cost. Their major disadvantage is their limited ability to address other, more deep-seated psychological problems of the recovering executive. Therapists will also differ greatly with regard to their interest in being in communication with the firm about the recovering executive's progress. As with the insight-oriented therapists, it is important to check on this issue in advance.

Medication Therapy

Medication therapy may play a significant role in the recovering executive's inpatient and aftercare treatment plans. Psychiatric medications are designed to return the disordered mental state of the individual to normal. They achieve this by relieving the acute symptoms of the psychiatric illness, stabilizing the patient's condition, and in some instances preventing the recurrence of the symptoms. The psychiatric medications achieve these effects by working at the neurochemical level to alter the quantity and interaction of the neurotransmitters, the basic chemical building blocks of the brain. In spite of their powerful effects, psychiatric medications do not cure psychiatric illness. Instead, they relieve the most debilitating signs and symptoms of mental distress. The vast majority of psychiatric medications are not addicting and have very little or no abuse potential. However, these medications are powerful and commonly have a number of side effects that must be monitored closely. In addition, not all psychiatric medications work with equal effectiveness in all individuals, for reasons that are not entirely clear. This makes it difficult to predict in advance which medication will ultimately be successful for a given patient's problem. It is not unusual for patients to be tried on a number of different medications at varying dosages before the right medication at the right dosage is discovered. Which medication a psychiatrist will ultimately recommend will depend on a complex set of factors, including diagnosis, outcome of previous medication therapy, psychiatric and medication histories of close relatives, potential for the appearance of side effects, the psychiatrist's experience with a particular drug, and the cost and availability of the medication.

The goal of the psychiatrist is to prescribe the appropriate medication in the lowest possible dosage that effectively removes the signs and symptoms of the illness while minimizing the appearance of side effects. If given in too high a dosage, many of these medications are toxic. How long a patient will have to remain on a given medication depends on the nature of the illness and its symptoms. The range can be from a few weeks to several years, and many patients are continued on their medication after they leave the hospital. Despite the care with which psychiatric medications are prescribed, medication failures are common. The causes of medication failure include the wrong diagnosis, the wrong dosage, lack of patient compliance, unacceptable level of side effects, and interference from other prescribed medications.

Antipsychotics and Antidepressants   The antipsychotics, also known as the major tranquilizers, were discovered in France in 1952. The first antipsychotic drug to achieve widespread use by the psychiatric community was chlorpromazine, or Thorazine. There are now a large number of these medications available on the market. The major classes of these drugs include the phenothiazines, butyrophenones, thioxanthenes, dibenzoxazepines, dihydroindolones, and rauwolfia alkaloids. Seventy percent of patients using the major tranquilizers gain significant relief, while only 10 percent are not helped (Kaplan and Sadock, 1981, p. 771). The antipsychotics are useful for a wide range of disorders, including schizophrenia, brief psychotic episodes, manic-depressive illness, drug-induced psychosis, psychotic depression, and chronic brain syndrome. They alleviate a variety of signs and symptoms, including auditory or visual hallucinations; delusional thinking; agitation; hostility; disorientation; and impairments in insight, judgment, memory, concentration, and attention span. The commonly used antipsychotics include Thorazine, Serentil, Mellaril, Prolixin, Trilafon, Stelazine, Taractan, Navane, Loxitane, Haldol, and Moban. When a patient is started on these medications, most of the improvement in his or her clinical condition occurs within the first six to eighteen weeks. These drugs have a variety of side effects, including sedation, tremors, muscle cramps and stiffness, blurriness of vision, dry mouth, light-headedness, constipation, urine retention, and allergic reactions. Many of these side effects clear up on their own or can be effectively controlled with other medications such as Benadryl, Cogentin, and Artane. A more serious consequence of ingestion of these medications is the development of tardive dyskinesia, an irreversible, late-occurring, and relatively rare neurological syndrome that is seen in a very small number of patients who have been taking antipsychotic medications for significant periods of time. The syndrome consists of involuntary movements of face, neck, and limbs. Unfortunately, there is no effective treatment at the current time.

The antidepressants were discovered in the late 1950s. The antidepressant medications, which are effective in relieving the signs and symptoms of depression, fall into two main categories: tricyclic antidepressants (TCAs) and monoamine oxidase inhibitors (MAOIs). Although both classes of medication are very effective in the treatment of depression, these drugs do not produce euphoria but instead simply return the depressed individual to a normal mood state. They also alleviate the signs and symptoms of depression, including poor appetite, agitation, anxiety, insomnia, low energy level, poor concentration, decreased attention span, poor memory, and feelings of helplessness and hopelessness. The side effects of these medications include sedation, tremors, blurriness of vision, dry mouth, light-headedness, constipation, urine retention, and allergic reactions. The MAOIs are considered to be not quite as effective as the trycyclic antidepressants. MAOIs have the additional disadvantage of requiring that the patient avoid certain foods that may adversely interact with them. The antidepressants commonly available are Elavil, Aventyl, Vivactil, Tofranil, Norpramin, Sinequan, Adapin, Asendin, Ludiomil, Desyrel, Marplan, Nardil, and Parnate.

What are the implications for a recovering executive who is prescribed one of the antipsychotic or antidepressant medications? First, for recovering executives who are used to a high level of mental acuity, the sedative properties of these medications can be quite a hindrance. Recovering executives should monitor their day-to-day sleep-wake cycle to determine at what time of the day they are most alert. They should then schedule those activities that require the greatest degree of concentration and mental alertness at those times. Second, it is important to remember that these drugs do not cure the underlying condition but only keep its symptoms under control. The executive who stops taking his or her medication for whatever reason can expect to see a return of the symptoms within varying periods of time. In addition, these medications are not like aspirin, which one takes when feeling ill. The maintenance of adequate blood levels of these medications is very important to their therapeutic effect. Taking them irregularly will significantly reduce their therapeutic action.

Lithium   The third class of psychiatric medications is lithium. Lithium carbonate was approved for use in the United States in 1970 and was found to be effective in the treatment of acute mania. It was also found to be effective in preventing relapses in both bipolar illness, including mania and depression, and recurrent unipolar depression. Lithium is a naturally occurring element. In therapeutic doses it is associated with a number of side effects, including stomach distress, fatigue and muscle tiredness, tremor of the hands, increased thirst and urination, weight gain, changes in thyroid function, EKG changes, and kidney problems. For executives the hand tremor can be the most distressing side effect, particularly in meetings. Fortunately, the tremor can be helped by another medication, Inderal. The concentration of lithium carbonate in the blood must remain within a very narrow range; lithium concentrations outside this range can be toxic. Lithium concentration is monitored by drawing blood samples at regular intervals. Checking lithium blood levels regularly may be particularly bothersome if the executive travels frequently. It is not uncommon for many post-discharge executives and other recovering manic individuals to complain that they feel that they are in a mental "straitjacket." They simply do not have their old level of energy. Unfortunately, there is little that can be done about this.

Antianxiety Agents   The fourth class of psychiatric medication includes the antianxiety agents. The antianxiety agents are used for acute anxiety, panic attacks, phobias, drug withdrawal, certain organic brain syndromes, and sleeping difficulties. The commonly prescribed antianxiety agents include Librium, Valium, Tranzene, Centrax, Paxipam, Ativan, Serax, and Xanax. At one time these agents were the most commonly prescribed medications in the United States. Unlike the other classes of psychiatric medications, agents in this class have a significant potential for abuse due to their ability to induce physiological and psychological dependence. As a consequence, these medications should only be viewed as short-term treatments to be used until the root causes of the patient's problems are uncovered. These medications are infrequently used as part of the aftercare plan for recovering individuals, and they are specifically counterindicated for recovering alcoholics and drug-dependent individuals.

References

American Psychiatric Association. *Diagnostic and Statistical Manual of Mental Disorders–III–Revised.* Washington, D.C.: American Psychiatric Association, 1987.

Bissell, L., and Jones, R. W. "The Alcoholic Nurse." *Nursing Outlook,* 1981, *29,* 96–101.

Blotnick, S. *The Corporate Steeplechase: Predictable Crisis in a Business Career.* New York: Facts on File, 1984.

Busch, L. "Rehabilitating the Impaired Dentist: A Look at What the Profession Is Doing to Help." *Journal of the American Medical Association,* 1982, *105,* 781–787.

Cooper, C. L., and Marshall, J. *Understanding Executive Stress.* New York: Petrocelli Books, 1977.

Cooper, C. L., and Payne, R. *Current Concerns in Occupational Stress.* New York: Wiley, 1980.

Frances, R. G., Alexopoulos, V., and Yandow, V. "Lawyers' Alcoholism." *Advances in Alcohol and Substance Abuse,* 1984, *4* (2), 59–66.

Goleman, D. "The Strange Agony of Success." *New York Times,* Aug. 24, 1986, sec. 3, Business, p. 1F.

Greiff, B. S., and Munter, P. K. *Executive, Family, and Organizational Life.* New York: New American Library, 1980.

Helfrich, A. A., Crowley, T. J., Atkinson, C. A., and Post, R. D. "A Clinical Profile of 136 Cocaine Abusers." In L. S. Harris (ed.), *Problems of Drug Dependence*. Washington, D.C.: U.S. Government Printing Office, National Institute on Drug Abuse Research Monograph, DHHS Pul. no. (ADM) 83-1264, 1982, pp. 343–350.

Kaplan, H. I., and Sadock, B. J. (eds.). *Modern Synopsis of Comprehensive Textbook of Psychiatry*, 3rd ed. Baltimore, Md.: Williams & Wilkins, 1981.

Kaplan, H. I., and Sadock, B. J. (eds.). *Comprehensive Textbook of Psychiatry*, 4th ed. Baltimore, Md.: Williams & Wilkins, 1985.

Kets de Vries, M.F.R., and Miller, D. *The Neurotic Organization: Diagnosing and Changing Counterproductive Styles of Management*. San Francisco: Jossey-Bass, 1984.

Kolb, L. B. *Modern Clinical Psychiatry*. Philadelphia: Saunders, 1977.

Kotter, J. P. *The General Managers*. New York: New Press, 1982.

Levinson, H. *Emotional Health: In the World of Work*. New York: Harper & Row, 1964.

Levinson, H. *Executive Stress*. New York: New American Library, 1975.

Levinson, H. *Executive*. Cambridge, Mass.: Harvard University Press, 1981.

McLean, A. *Occupational Stress*. Springfield, Ill.: Thomas, 1974.

Maccoby, M. *Leader*. New York: Simon & Schuster, 1981.

Masi, D. A. *Designing Employee Assistance Programs*. New York: American Management Associations, 1984.

Mirin, S. M. (ed.). *Substance Abuse and Psychopathology*. Washington, D.C.: American Psychiatric Press, 1984.

Nicholi, A. M. *The New Harvard Guide to Psychiatry*. Cambridge, Mass.: Harvard University Press, 1988.

Rohrlich, J. B. *Work and Love: The Crucial Balance*. New York: Harmony Books, 1980.

Schuckit, M. A. "Cocaine and the Clinician." *Psychiatric Times*, Nov. 1968, *111* (11), 4–5.

Shain, M., and Groeneveld, J. *Employee Assistance Programs: Philosophy, Theory and Practice*. Lexington, Mass.: LexingtonBooks, D. C. Heath, 1980, p. 126.

Stimmel, B. (ed.). *Alcohol and Drug Abuse in the Affluent*. New York: Haworth Press, 1984.

Torrey, E. F. *Surviving Schizophrenia.* New York: Harper & Row, 1983.

Trice, H. M., and Beyer, J. M. "Differential Use of an Alcoholism Policy in Federal Organizations by Skill Level of Employees." In C. J. Schramm (ed.), *Alcoholism and Its Treatment in Industry.* Baltimore, Md.: Johns Hopkins University Press, 1977.

Vaillant, G. E. *The Natural History of Alcoholism: Causes, Patterns, and Paths to Recovery.* Cambridge, Mass.: Harvard University Press, 1983.

Waldinger, R. J. *Fundamentals of Psychiatry.* Washington, D.C.: American Psychiatric Press, 1986.

Index

Adapin, 152
Admissions process, 92–93
Adult Children of Alcoholics, 102
Affective disorders, 15, 52, 63. *See also* Depression; Manic-depressive illness
AFL-CIO, 27
Aftercare planning, 100–101, 102–103
Age: alcoholism and, 17; depression and, 57
AIDS, 47
Al-Anon, 102, 104
Alcohol: depression and, 16–17, 60, 61, 62; impairment of job performance and, 30–34; manic-depressive illness and, 63, 70; physical effects of, 27, 31; tolerance for, 28
Alcoholics Anonymous, 23, 102–103, 126, 140, 148
Alcoholism: case studies of, 22–35, 139–141; causes of, 15–17; consequences of, 24, 27–28; definition of, 24; denial of, 30; depression and, 51; development of, 24–26; as disease, 26–29, 35; examples of, 8, 23–24; myths of, 29–33; other illnesses and, 27, 31; personality changes and, 33;

physical signs of, 34–35; psychological impairments and, 31–32; "social" drinking and, 33; symptoms of, 33–35; treatment of, 32; willpower and, 29–30; withdrawal problems of, 26, 28–29
American Board of Neurology and Psychiatry, 119
American Hospital Association, 27
American Medical Association, 27
American Psychiatric Association, 11, 80
Amnestic syndrome, 15
Amphetamines, 38, 39, 43, 82, 83
Angel dust, 45
Antianxiety agents, 44, 153–154
Antidepressants, 56, 152–153
Antipsychotics, 151–153
Artane, 152
Asendin, 152
Ativan, 154
Atkinson, C. A., 37
Aventyl, 152

Barbitone, 44
Barbiturates, 42, 43–44
Behavioral therapy, 125, 149–150
Benadryl, 152
Benzedrine, 43
Beyer, J. M., 3

159